D0848803

NO LONGER PROPERTY OF
BRESCIA COLLEGE LIBRARY

The Catholic Cult of the Paraclete

The Catholic Cult of the Paraclete

By

JOSEPH H. FICHTER

With a Foreword by
DONALD L. GELPI

SHEED and WARD, INC.
Subsidiary of Universal Press Syndicate
NEW YORK

BRESCIA COLLEGE LIBRARY
OWENSBORO, KENTUCKY

301.242
F445

The Catholic Cult of the Paraclete. Copyright © 1975 by Joseph H. Fichter. All rights reserved. Printed in the United States of America. No part of this book may be used or reproduced in any manner whatsoever without written permission except in the case of reprints in the context of reviews. For information write Sheed and Ward, Inc. 475 Fifth Avenue, New York, N.Y. 10017.

Library of Congress Catalog Card Number 74-10163
ISBN: 0-8362-0599-5

Contents

69798

69798,

FOREWORD

The apostle Paul counseled the church at Thessolonika to test all things and hold on to what is good. And to judge from his letters to the charismatic, eucharistic communities he founded, he set rather high standards for "goodness."

There were no Catholic sociologists around when Paul wrote. But we do know that he was mightily concerned to remain factually informed of developments in the churches under his care. It is not, then, wholly fanciful to imagine that had Paul had access to a competent sociologist, he would have put him to good pastoral use in the exercise of his apostolate.

Concern with facts is the business of sociologists. And professional concern with getting at the facts about the Church has been one of the lifelong passions of Father Joseph Fichter, S.J. As a result, it would be difficult to find a Catholic sociologist with professional and personal authority and credentials to match those which Father Fichter brings to the present study. It is therefore an important scholarly contribution to the growing body of literature surrounding the Catholic charismatic renewal.

The Catholic charismatic renewal is, despite its rapid numerical expansion, still in the early stages of development as a movement. Those who are concerned with its healthy growth in the future and with its impact on the Church as a whole would, then, do well to study and ponder prayerfully the implications of Father Fichter's survey of lay, charismatic Catholics. It is a carefully documented and nuanced portrait of forces and tensions that are shaping Catholic charismatic piety. This study is honestly sensitive to the positive values that are present in the renewal: its authentic religiosity, the sense of new life and of personal regeneration it has brought to thousands of Catholics, the strong sense of community and of sharing in faith the graces and gifts of God. At the same time, Father Fichter's survey has laid bare with a certain documented objectivity some of the pastoral problems which have emerged in charismatic prayer communities. No one familiar with the letters of Paul should be surprised to discover that such pastoral problems exist. But when one is dealing with a movement as widespread as the charismatic renewal, it is sometimes difficult to come to anything more than an intuitive sense of the pastoral drift of things.

From the standpoint of charismatic piety, Father Fichter's study of the renewal is, then, a remarkable exercise in spiritual discernment. I know that it has been not only professionally but prayerfully done. And it should be a witness to charismatic Catholics of how the power of the Spirit can transform from within the processes of sociological research.

Father Fichter's study portrays a movement that is humanly, theologically, and spiritually pluralistic. Through a skillful balancing of statistical data and direct quotation, he gives the reader a clear sense of the many cultural and regional variables which lend diversity to the charismatic movement in America. And he gives a vital sense of the human, religious, and pastoral concerns which characterize those involved in charismatic prayer communities.

Father Fichter has, then, sketched with masterful skill a descriptive portrait of a significant and expanding movement which is still in the early stages of its growth and development. The charismatic renewal emerges from these pages as a movement still concerned to find complete acceptance by the Church universal. It is a movement in tension between its early originating experiences and its growing national and international impact. It is a movement stretched between ecumenical openness and a concern with orthodoxy. It is a movement still groping for a satisfactory formula that effectively coordinates its lay and clerical leadership. It is a movement caught between its fear of institutional fossilization and the need to establish social structures to deal with pastoral problems of increasing complexity. It is a movement that is encumbered by muddled and fundamentalistic God-talk while groping for new formulas for articulating its religious experience.

Father Fichter argues persuasively that the Catholic charismatic renewal is at present a cult, not a sect, within the Church universal. Some charismatic Catholics may balk at such a dispassionate sociological labeling of an intensely meaningful religious experience, but Father Fichter's point remains, nonetheless, completely valid.

From a theological rather than a sociological standpoint, however, it is worth remarking that there are cults and cults. Any authentic Christian cult will place special values and importance on one or other aspect of a Christian faith experience. The aspect singled out as the focus of special attention and devotion may be more or less central to Christian life and worship. Some cults, like that dedicated to devotion to the Sacred Heart, have, with time, been recommended by official Church teachers as not only dogmatically sound but rooted in the most basic Christian beliefs and attitudes.

Certainly, there are aspects of Catholic charismatic piety which are expressive of what is fundamental in Christian life and faith: personal conversion to Christ, openness to the Spirit and to his gifts, love of Scripture, and the sharing of charismatic graces in mutual faith and love. These things ought to be perennial endowments of any believing, vital Christian community. Moreover, no one can read the documents of Vatican II without acknowledging that they have already been sanctioned by the official pastoral magisterium. Yet, one may be hard put at times to find overt signs of their presence among "non-charismatic" Roman Catholics.

Father Fichter's study also documents the fact, however, that along with such basic Christian attitudes, charismatic Catholics show symptoms of religious inauthenticity and inconsistency. And it is to these points especially that those concerned with the healthy growth and development of the Catholic charismatic renewal would do well to attend most carefully. One would hope that the leadership of the movement would react to them, not defensively, but creatively and pastorally.

Father Fichter's survey has uncovered three symptoms of "heterodoxy" among charismatic Catholics. It is useful to note that "heterodoxy" functions in the text more as a sociological than a theological term, although it has theological connotations. In its sociological use "heterodox" designates factual differences in belief and prescinds from the larger theological question of what a given religious group ought to believe.

The three areas of sociological "heterodoxy" which Father

Fichter's survey uncovers are the following. A significant number of the lay Catholics surveyed subscribe to belief in an imminent second coming. They have a conviction that they are personally saved. And they are inclined to trust the heart rather than the head in religious matters.

Charismatic piety, in contrast to "traditional" Roman Catholic piety, is biblically based, and one of the problems which the writers of the New Testament had to resolve was the disappointment of their expectations that the second coming of Christ would occur relatively soon after the first. One might argue that much popular Roman Catholic piety has not in the past been sufficiently eschatological in its tone. But while Catholics may have something to learn from Protestants in matters eschatological, not every form of eschatological expectation is authentically Christian.

Father Fichter's findings suggest that a significant number of Catholic charismatics are in fact imbibing an unhealthy and fundamentalistic form of eschatology. Expectation of the second coming becomes distorted when it becomes an excuse for refusing to commit oneself in atoning love to this world. The presence of such a belief among a significant number of charismatic Catholics becomes particularly unsettling when it is linked to the general absence of social involvement on their part. Father Fichter's study documents the presence of both tendencies among Catholic charismatics.

If, then, the Catholic charismatic renewal is genuinely concerned to find acceptance by the universal Church, it would do well to transform its growing enthusiasm for an imminent Parousia into practical social and political concern for the suffering, the outcast, and the oppressed. Unless charismatic Catholics do so, their cries of "maranatha" will have an increasingly hollow ring in the ears of their fellow Christians.

Father Fichter has also documented the need for a correc-

tive catechesis in what touches belief in personal salvation.
Those pastorally involved in the renewal would, no doubt,
be able to extend the list of dogmatic confusions on the basis
of their personal and pastoral experience. Conviction of
personal salvation was originally linked with the doctrine
of predestination, and it was accordingly rejected by the
official pastoral catechesis. Although Protestant pentecostals
sometimes indulge in a rhetoric colored by their Calvinist
heritage, they do not as a group subscribe to a strict pre-
destinationist doctrine. For the Protestant pentecostal to
say that he is "saved" often means little more than that he
has accepted the grace and salvation Jesus brings. Still, the
widespread indulgence by Catholic charismatics in confused
and potentially misleading soteriological rhetoric ought to
be a source of genuine pastoral concern to leaders in the
renewal.

The tendency of Catholic charismatics to value the heart
over the mind raises more philosophical than theological
issues. If in the past Protestant pentecostals have tended to
exaggerate the place of emotion in religion, one can find
equally unhealthy symptoms of rationalism among Roman
Catholics. Father Fichter holds up the sound integration
of mind and heart as the only viable ideal in such matters,
and he correctly calls into question the signs of anti-intellectualism among Catholic charismatics.

Finally, Father Fichter's survey has documented the
existence of socially liberal attitudes among charismatic
Catholics as well as a serious lack of active social involvement
on their part. And he has also documented the tendency of
charismatic Catholics to use a fundamentalistic rhetoric
to avoid facing current social and moral questions. Certainly
one of the problems present in charismatic prayer groups
is the penchant of some charismatics to indulge in a kind

of God-talk that all but obliterates concern with the limiting human and environmental variables which function in a given religious situation. Leaders in the charismatic renewal would, then, do well to become better informed concerning the social and moral issues facing our nation and others. And they would do well to seek prayerfully the means to channel the religious enthusiasm of local prayer groups into a concern for meeting those needs.

In other words, Father Fichter's study documents the fact that if the Catholic charismatic renewal is to find a more general acceptance among Catholics and if it is to have the impact on the universal Church which it presently seeks, it will have to do a certain amount of pastoral and spiritual housecleaning first. It seems to me unlikely that charismatic Catholics will be able to come to terms effectively with whatever inauthenticities are now present in their piety without the help, teaching, and counsel of the rest of the Church. Moreover, as devoted members of that Church they have the right in strict justice and charity to find such help. Those who attend prayer meetings have no monopoly on the gifts of the Spirit. It is only by openness to the spiritual gifts operative in the universal Church that any individual or group within the Christian community comes to adequate spiritual balance.

At the same time, when one surveys the spiritual desiccation and apathy of large segments of the institutional Church, there can be little doubt that in their loyalty to Christ and his Church, in their conviction of God's saving power, in their enthusiasm for the word of God, in their thirst for teaching and spiritual growth, charismatic Catholics are being blessed by the Spirit with gifts which the rest of the community desperately needs.

Despite the presence of salutary cautions in the pages

which follow, this book ought, then, to be a source of genuine encouragement to Catholic charismatics. Father Fichter's survey should lay to rest the lurking fears which anyone may still have about the divisive intent of the Catholic charismatic renewal. Catholic charismatics are not in desire and aspiration a divisive, splintering sect within the Church. Those involved in the renewal give evidence of being deeply and genuinely loyal to the institutional Church. And they are looking to the institutional Church for guidance and direction.

Moreover, the pages which follow help to clarify the areas in which those in the renewal need most guidance. The most obvious need is for competent teachers to counteract those fundamentalistic tendencies in the renewal which are the consequence of ignorance and of premature and undirected ecumenical contacts. It is my personal conviction that the needed guidance can only be provided adequately by the local parish. There is, then, a genuine need for existing prayer communities to be thoroughly integrated into the life of each local parish. In the process, the renewal may be able to achieve a more realistic coordination of clerical and lay leadership.

Whether the institutional Church will show sufficient flexibility and pastoral wisdom in dealing with charismatic Catholics still remains to be seen. There are, however, many heartening signs that more and more official Church leaders are becoming pastorally sensitive both to the values in charismatic forms of prayer and to the pastoral needs of charismatic Catholics.

One can only hope that Father Fichter and others like him will continue to keep a weather eye on further developments in the charismatic renewal. I am myself very grateful for having had the opportunity to cooperate with him in the present study. May the spiritual wisdom and insight in these pages act as a leaven in the renewal and in those it touches.

Donald L. Gelpi, S.J.
JESUIT SCHOOL OF THEOLOGY AT BERKELEY

1

The Sociological Level

In the dim past of a generation or more ago there were people who felt that the sociologist was impertinent, if not meddlesome, when he dared to apply his profane methodology to the study of religious behavior and groups. There are two assumptions underlying this negative attitude. The first is the widespread notion that religion is an exclusively personal experience, a relationship with God that transcends the bounds of social science. The second is the belief that there is nothing the sociologist can do that cannot be done better by theologians, canon lawyers, and moral philosophers.

When H. Paul Douglass, a pioneer in the sociological research of Protestant congregations, founded the Institute of Social and Religious Research after World War I, he aroused opposition from religionists and was continually under suspicion. Many of his fellow Protestants believed that "religion consists of direct and unique relations between God and the individual." When these individuals associate with others in the name of religion, they do so as an "essen-

1

tially spiritual entity, and only very secondarily as a social institution."[1]

This so-called Protestant doctrine—that the Church founded by Christ is "purely internal and spiritual in nature"—was cited also by a Catholic critic of the sociology of religion. According to this version it is possible to study sociologically the visible and external structures of Protestantism because they are secular (and not religious). Catholicism, however, the "society of true religion," was externally and visibly founded by Christ and is by its divine nature supernatural and sacred. Since there is nothing secular about the Catholic Church, it is not amenable to the secular methodology of social science.[2]

The associates and students of H. Paul Douglass continued the sociological research of Protestant religious bodies and organized a Religious Research Fellowship at a time when there were relatively few systematic efforts to sociologize the American Catholic Church.[3] From the point of view of ecclesiastical authority, these Catholic research efforts were not legitimized until 1965 when the American hierarchy promoted the establishment (without financing it) of the Center for Applied Research in the Apostolate (CARA) in Washington, D.C. In that same year the delegates to the Second Vatican Council approved a document which encouraged and "cordially recommended" sociological surveys of the Catholic Church.[4]

The present sociological study represents our attempt to follow this high recommendation and to acknowledge the encouragement of several priest-leaders of the charismatic renewal. There are probably some conscientious religionists who are convinced that "the objective study of religion is at best impossible, and at worst dangerous," but the pentecostal leaders are not among them. On the other hand, there are probably only a few social scientists who still think that "everything important about religion is available to the objective observer,"[5] but the present writer is not among them. Any movement for religious change and renewal ought to be open to, and perhaps benefit from, sociological interpretation.

Sociologizing the Spiritual

Since Vatican II, Catholics at all levels of the Church have been preoccupied with aggiornamento, and much of the emphasis has been on organizational and structural problems: the revamping of the Vatican Curia, the establishment of episcopal synods, pastoral councils and associations of clergy and religious women, and the encouragement of coresponsibility and collegiality in the affairs of the Church. There are astute observers, however, who feel that this emphasis has been misplaced and that structural reform is not nearly so important as personal reform.

One of the leading pentecostal spokesmen, Donald Gelpi, remarks that "one cannot renew a church simply by reforming its structures, however important such reforms are for the gradual transformation of popular religious attitudes. For unless we are also willing to rend our hearts and rely on the grace of God, rending our institutional garments and restructuring them will in the long run accomplish little enough for the kingdom of God."[6] Sociologists have looked extensively at the efforts to restructure the "institutional garments" of the Catholic Church, and are now turning to the sociological aspects of the charismatic movement.

The Catholic pentecostal renewal may be seen as an effort to cut through these external and structural matters, and to turn "inward" to the essential spiritual and functional aspects of religion. Pope Paul VI suggested this change of

3

emphasis when he said that it would be an "error of method" to limit ourselves to the purely sociological level of studying the Church. He reminds us that "it is God who takes the initiative and has the principal role. Man's part, while necessary and not merely passive, still is rather one of disposing himself and cooperating with God."[7] The time has come to concentrate on the deeply spiritual and personal level of church life.

This emphasis on the spiritual was reinforced by Cardinal Suenens, who had been widely acclaimed as the principal proponent of structural reforms—of reorganizing the Church from the Roman Curia down to the local parish. He observed that structural changes have "merely reached the sociological level, not the spiritual. The people in these structures need to be alive in the Holy Spirit and sensitive to his action if they are truly to promote life, and not merely engage in sterile confrontation and the exchange of human opinion."[8] If the spiritual level is above and beyond the sociological level, is it then useless, or perhaps inappropriate, to attempt a sociological survey of people who are participating in the charismatic renewal?

The pentecostal theologian Edward O'Connor is sure that "a survey would miss the essence of the Pentecostal movement," because it presents statistics instead of persons, and generalizations instead of stories. He says that "the very point of this movement is the personal intervention of God in the lives of his people."[9] Yet he struggles with sociological terminology when he tries to avoid calling this collective phenomenon an organization, a structure, or even a movement. "It did not originate by the deliberate adoption of any goal, is not an organized enterprise, and does not consist in a method."[10] The findings of this survey will necessarily repudiate this observation. It must be stated clearly that

4

we are not trying to give a natural explanation for a supernatural phenomenon. We have no way of measuring the power of the Spirit. One married woman in New Jersey tells us that "the Spirit who lives in us cannot be categorized or punched on an IBM card. He lives and breathes where He will in those who have experienced in some way His powerful and loving action." A young man from Texas writes that "the Charismatic Renewal doesn't fit on computer programs. It's a living, loving, organic creation." A young teacher's aide in Pennsylvania remarks that "this is not a movement or an experience. What I've found is Church, real Christianity, a way of life."

The ascetical writers and mystics, who are now widely read by Catholic pentecostals, tell us that in the prayerful human relationship with God some people are still in the purgative way, others are in the illuminative way, and the more blessed are in the unitive way.[11] We do not know how to construct and employ empirically such ascetical categories. Nevertheless, what people say about themselves in this regard may well be the subject of sociological investigation, as indicated in a survey of "mystical experiences" conducted by Andrew Greeley and his associates.[12]

It would be futile for a sociologist of religion to attempt either to disprove or to demonstrate that the contemporary charismatic renewal was instituted by the Holy Spirit. This is not a sociological question: it cannot be investigated on a sociological level, nor can it be handled with the research tools available to social science. It is true that social scientists have studied the cultural conditions under which religious movements begin and flourish, as well as the types of people who are attracted to such movements. There is a large literature of this kind which attempts cultural and sometimes psychological explanations of why people get involved in

5

religious collectivities.[13] For the most part, however, these studies bypass the matter of divine origins and revelations, except to report what the participants believe.

Spiritual Counter-Culture

The sociologist is constrained to look for explanations of social behavior on a "this-worldly" level even while he does not deny or repudiate the supernatural and spiritual explanations given by the adherents of religious movements. What is probably the most fascinating and challenging aspect of Catholic pentecostalism is that it came as a surprise to sociologists of religion. We had studied the so-called religious revival as a statistical phenomenon of church membership during and after the Second World War, while at the same time witnessing a long-term trend toward secularization. It may well be that the lower-class Protestant denominations, conservative and pentecostal, represented a counter-trend to materialism and secularism, but no one expected an elaborately liturgical, sacramental, and hierarchical religion like Catholicism to imitate them.

If we can contrast institutional and structural reform with charismatic and personal renewal within the Catholic Church, we must contrast also the prevailing sensate American culture with the spiritual counter-culture represented by this contemporary religious movement. One of the frequent expressions of the movement's leadership is "we've got to build a new society within the shell of the old." This is an effort not to Christianize the socio-cultural system, but to set up a cultural environment within, along side of, and essentially counter to the secular culture. "We need to find a way of providing for people an authentically Christian environment of sufficient strength to make it possible for them to live as vital Christians if they so choose."[14]

6

Seeing this contrast in another way, Ralph Martin is convinced that the "worldly wisdom" of natural and scientific approaches "ends up missing the most important point, that the source of man's problems is spiritual at its core and can't be dealt with except in a spiritual way; and not simply a spiritual way of man's choosing, but *The Way* of God's choosing."[15] The promise of a worldly paradise achievable through technological development, scientific know-how, and social welfare has not been fulfilled. Catholic pentecostals are impressed with Karl Rahner's vision of the future Church that will diminish to a "little flock" existing in diaspora everywhere. One can hear the voice of Pitirim Sorokin echoing through these lamentations for a culture mired deeply in sensate, secular, and materialistic values.

There is general recognition among American sociologists of a long-term trend toward secularization—although Andrew Greeley raises a dissenting voice because he does not agree with the concomitant generalization concerning the decline of religion.[16] There is no doubt in the minds of Catholic pentecostals that the American culture is thoroughly secularized, indeed so corrupt and incorrigible that it is beyond regeneration. They would agree with Martin Marty that the Holy Spirit has an "errand" to perform within Christianity even if the American culture at large has rejected the Paraclete.[17]

It is probably not inappropriate to note that there are other organized efforts in search of a counter-culture. It is what the blacks are seeking in place of a white American culture that has no "soul." The Women's Liberation Movement expresses great dissatisfaction with the persistent manifestations of discrimination and injustice at all levels of society. There are those who feel that the "new generation" has found its soul in Consciousness III, which emphasizes self-renewal, authenticity, responsibility, love, and liberation. The various efforts to establish communes, many of them with no apparent religious inspiration, suggest a desire to flee the prevailing culture, and the increasing popularity among the young of eastern religions and transcendental philosophies is also indicative of the need for a counter-culture.[18]

Sociological studies of Catholic pentecostalism may be more useful to social science than to religion. The fact that a cult of this kind can flourish within the established *ecclesia*, that it does not seem to exhibit serious separatist tendencies, and that it gains its membership mainly from among bettereducated and middle-class Catholics constitutes a contemporary phenomenon that was unexpected by sociologists of religion. This was simply not the direction in which the post-conciliar Church was moving. In fact, the charismatic renewal represents a change of direction in that the religious experiences it encourages, such as the revival of bible reading, the open manifestation of religious emotions, and the deepening realization of God's providence in everyday life, are quite opposite in nature to both structural reform in the Church and the anticipated process of secularization in the culture.

Charismatic Structures

There is a reluctance on the part of sociologists to delve into the personal spiritual experience of individuals unless such experience is shared by others. We know from their own words that something interior and spiritual is happening to these people. Mystical contemplation is an individual, not a social, experience but it may happen to many in a similar way, and may thus become a behavior pattern for all members of the prayer community. There is no reason to doubt the young production engineer who says, "my involvement in the charismatic renewal has completely changed my life. I strongly and faithfully believe the Lord is moving me in his own way according to his will." A middle-aged postal worker from Nebraska exclaims that "baptism in the Holy Spirit and charismatic renewal are the closest thing next to heaven that a person can experience here on earth."

When large numbers of people reveal such similar experiences we recognize a shared or collective pattern of behavior which must obviously be treated as a sociological phenomenon. In the questionnaire used in our survey we asked about the background experiences and attitudes of Catholic lay adults in the movement. To the extent that these phenomena are similar and shared we are able to deal with them at the sociological level. We shall see that the members are more interested in personal conversion than in social reform: they feel that church renewal—structural and functional—must emerge from personal renewal. Nevertheless, in manifesting these individualistic beliefs and practices collectively, they are subject to sociological research.

The unwillingness of Catholic pentecostals to speak of the charismatic renewal as a movement or organization seems to stem from a reluctance to admit that religious spontaneity ineluctably becomes institutionalized, that groups of people assembling for spiritual purposes have to develop social structures. Patterns of prayer and worship, by the mere fact of frequent repetition, take on an accepted and approved uniformity. Primary relationships among people in the group, at first informal, personal, and face-to-face, become formalized and standardized. The format of the prayer meeting has become typical, so that a member knows what to expect when visiting a prayer group anywhere in the country.[19]

We shall see that the pentecostal movement among Catholics must be sociologically defined as a religious cult, rather than a religious sect, a form the movement took among lower-class Protestants. The local prayer group must not be confused with the so-called "underground church," a fact that was demonstrated in the study of comparative groups in New Jersey by Meredith McGuire.[20] In our survey we found that less than 4% of the respondents had ever been connected with an underground church. On the other hand, however, the charismatic group must not be confused with conventional parish "societies" like the Sodality of Our Lady, the Holy Name Society, and the Parents' Club. Indeed, we found that two-thirds of the respondents meet in prayer groups that are not located in their home parish. All of these comparative data underscore the fact that the charismatic renewal can be sociologically identified as a form of organized collectivity.

The local prayer communities are not really autonomous and isolated from the network of similar groups around the country. There are city-wide days of renewal and occasional diocesan and regional conferences that require organized planning and communication. Gerlach and Hine remark that "the concept of individual access to the spiritual source of authority, when taken seriously, tends to prevent organizational solidarity and centralized control." They suggest that the pentecostal movement, as a whole, tends to be both acephalous and reticulate, but they recognize an "infrastructure" of personal relations, leadership exchange, and traveling evangelists.[21]

Taken in its totality on the American scene, Catholic pentecostalism exhibits all the essential elements of a large-scale organization. It contains a power structure of decision makers at all levels, even though terms like "discernment" and "authority of service" are the preferable descriptions.

"Because the charismatic renewal is a renewal (an unorganized movement) there can be no authority structure within it. The only authority can be the authority that comes from service well performed."[22] There are group goals, and these are the fulfillment of the will of God. There are typical channels of communication, which are thought of as means of "sharing" with the members. The usual differentiation of roles, or division of labor, is demonstrated in the various "ministries." The recognition of these organizational elements does not secularize or profane the charismatic renewal. It simply indicates that sacred and religious movements are structured around normal human behavior, and are thus researchable at the sociological level.

The leaders of the movement seem to have no antipathy to sociological analysis, nor do they fear a survey. I was invited to present reports on the research findings to local meetings and diocesan conferences, as well as to the International Conference at the University of Notre Dame, and these were duly described in *New Covenant*. The well-known Word of God community at Ann Arbor showed no hesitancy in cooperating with a sociological investigator in 1969.[23] The study of lay charismatics on which we are here reporting was begun and conducted with the enthusiastic support of Harold Cohen, Donald Gelpi, and others in the New Orleans prayer community who reviewed the pretest questionnaire and each succeeding phase of the research program.

Why Only Lay Catholics?

When presenting papers and leading discussions on this research survey, I have frequently been asked why I excluded Protestants, priests, sisters, brothers, seminarians, and students from the study. The main reason is that charis-

11

matic renewal is largely a movement of the laity within the Church. As Kilian McDonnell remarked, "the movement is dominantly lay in character. The theology and rhetoric are essentially lay." He added that "it would be a sad day if the movement were to become clericalized and lose its lay character."[24] The original impetus came from lay persons at Duquesne University and at South Bend and Ann Arbor. The Charismatic Communication Center at Notre Dame is operated by laymen; the movement's periodical, *New Covenant*, is managed and edited by laymen. The so-called Service Committee, established in 1970, was composed of five laymen and two priests.[25]

Although the Catholic clergy and religious sisters and brothers are attracted in growing numbers to the charismatic renewal, the organizers and managers of the movement, as well as the great majority of its membership, are lay people. With the limited research funds at our disposal we felt that we could obtain significant results by concentrating exclusively on the lay adult membership, thus allowing other interested researchers to extend their studies to other categories of members. "Captive audiences" of student prayer groups are easily accessible to sociologists on college campuses, and they have attracted research attention. There appears to be little systematic study, however, of the many Protestants who attend Catholic prayer meetings.

The present study focuses only on Catholic lay adults, but there is no way of knowing how many are involved in the movement in America. No roster of the lay membership exists, and the only usable source for the construction of a sample was the listing of prayer groups in the 1972 *Directory*, published by the Charismatic Communication Center at the University of Notre Dame.[26] With some exceptions, each entry indicates the percentage of Catholics in the group, the name and telephone number of the contact person, and the place and time of prayer meetings.[27] Since we wanted to survey only Catholics, we took our sample only from groups that reported more than 50% Catholic membership, of which there were 464. From these we selected every third group, and with some difficulty verified the name and address from the *Official Catholic Directory* of 1972 (usually through the nearest Catholic parish or school).[28]

While the respondents to this survey are fairly well distributed by states and regions according to the location of prayer groups around the country, they do not constitute a cross section, or random sample, representative of lay Catholic charismatics—nor were they intended to do so. There are unquestionably more women than men in the movement, but we deliberately asked for three men and three women from each group. In total then, we have responses from 375 men and 369 women.

One other aspect of this survey prevents it from being a random scientific sample representative of the total population of adult Catholic lay charismatics—the fact that we had no control over the selection of persons to whom the questionnaires were given. We assume that the contact persons, or group leaders, chose the "better," or more faithful and knowledgeable members to answer the questionnaires. If this assumption is correct, we must conclude that this survey has reached the more active and dedicated of the laity involved in charismatic renewal, and relatively few of the rank-and-file membership.

The listing of the nine regions of the country in Table 1.1 follows the divisions used by the United States Census Bureau, and used also by the *Official Catholic Directory*. The two regions with the highest Catholic population, the Middle Atlantic States and the East North Central States,

TABLE 1.1

Regional Distribution and Percentage Response of Catholic Pentecostal Groups Sampled

Region	GROUPS		QUESTIONNAIRES	
	% Distribution (n = 464)	% Sampled (n = 155)	% Mailed (n = 930)	% Returned (n = 744)
New England	7.3	8.4	8.4	7.9
Middle Atlantic	21.8	21.9	21.9	22.5
South Atlantic	7.9	10.3	10.3	10.0
East North Central	27.6	24.5	24.5	24.9
East South Central	2.1	1.9	1.9	2.4
West North Central	10.7	11.0	11.0	11.4
West South Central	9.8	11.0	11.0	10.6
Mountain States	5.1	4.5	4.5	4.3
Pacific States	7.7	6.5	6.5	6.0

are also the areas where the largest number of Catholic charismatic prayer groups are located. They are also the regions from which we received the highest proportions of returned questionnaires.

Locating the Charismatics

The decision to conduct a survey of charismatic Catholic lay people was reached in consultation with Harold Cohen, Donald Gelpi, Henry Montecino, and Louis Poché, who are priest-leaders in the flourishing New Orleans Charismatic Community. With their advice the questionnaire schedule was composed, pretested, and revised several times. A modest Faculty Research Grant was provided by Loyola University, and the research facilities of the Department of Sociology were made available. The one-third sample of Catholic Prayer Groups was drawn from the 1972 *Directory,* and the addresses were verified tentatively by the beginning of December.

We then mailed a double postcard to the contact person in each of the 155 charismatic prayer groups that made up the original sample. This postcard asked whether the leader was willing to distribute six questionnaires to adult lay members, three to males and three to females. Thirty-two of these groups (20.6%) had to be replaced by others: five of them had only women members; two were made up of seminarians; one was a Spanish-speaking group; and five had contact persons who could not be reached because they were men who had left the priesthood. One of these ex-priests returned the postcard with the notation: "I am no longer a member of the Roman Church." The remaining nineteen simply did not answer the postcard.

At intervals of three weeks until the middle of March we followed up, or replaced, those groups which either did not fit the conditions of the sample or did not respond to our postcard.[29] In order to keep the regional distribution of the sample in proper balance, we chose replacements from the same state, when there were available addresses, or from the adjoining state in the region, when there were not. At final count the contact persons or leaders who accepted the responsibility of distributing questionnaires to their members included fifty-seven priests, twenty-seven sisters, eleven brothers, thirty-five laymen, nineteen laywomen, and six married couples.[30]

Table 1.2 subsumes the nine census regions into four sections of the country according to the formula used by the Gallup Organization and other professional pollsters. This redistribution shows that we were able to reach more than one-third of the prayer groups in the East and the South, but less than one-third in the Midwest and the West. While an 80% return rate is highly satisfactory for any mailed survey, we note that the return rate was lower than this in the South and the West. Nevertheless, we may feel confident that the 744 respondents represent a fairly well-balanced regional distribution.

There are eight states in which we reached no Catholic lay charismatics. Two of them, Alaska and Idaho, had no Catholic prayer group listed in the 1972 *Directory*. Six other states had Catholic groups from whom we received no responses; they are Kentucky, Nevada, North Carolina, Oklahoma, Oregon, and Utah. Seven states, however, each having twenty-five or more prayer groups, contributed the largest

TABLE 1.2

Four-Region Distribution of Pentecostal Groups and of Questionnaires Mailed and Returned

| Region | GROUPS | | QUESTIONNAIRES | | |
	Number of Groups	Groups Sampled	Number Mailed	Number Returned	Return Rate
East	143	51	306	249	81.4%
Midwest	179	55	330	270	81.8%
South	82	32	192	148	77.1%
West	60	17	102	77	75.5%
Totals	464	155	930	744	80.0%

TABLE 1.3

Regional Percentage Distribution of Dioceses, Pentecostal Groups, and Respondents

Region	% Catholic Dioceses (n = 165)	% Dioceses Sampled (n = 88)	% Catholic Groups (n = 464)	% Groups Sampled (n = 155)	% Respondents (n = 744)
East	22.7	28.4	30.8	32.9	33.5
Midwest	35.1	35.2	38.6	35.5	36.3
South	22.7	22.7	17.7	20.6	19.9
West	19.5	13.6	12.9	11.0	10.3

number of answered questionnaires. Ranked by numbers of groups, they are New York, Illinois, Michigan, New Jersey, California, Texas, and Wisconsin.

The charismatic members responding from these prayer groups are located in eighty-eight of the 165 dioceses of the United States. The groups from which we received answered questionnaires are located in 57% of the dioceses in the Midwest and the South, but in 71% of the dioceses in the East, and only 40% of the dioceses in the West.

The data in Table 1.3 show that the largest numbers of Catholic dioceses, prayer groups, and charismatic lay people are located in the Midwest, while the smallest are found in the West. The apparent oversampling of dioceses in the East and undersampling of dioceses in the West simply reflect the fact that the charismatic movement is stronger, and the membership more numerous, in some dioceses than in others. There are fewer Catholics in the South and the West than in the two other sections of the country, and this accounts

17

69798   301.242
F445

Brescia College Library
Owensboro, Kentucky

for the lower proportion of both charismatic groups and individuals in those areas. The slightly lower response rate, as shown in Table 1.2, does not seem to be a significant factor in these regional distributions.

This brief description of the ordinary mechanics of a sociological survey tells us nothing more than the fact that the profane approach of social science may be of some utility to a religious movement. From this point of view, the general purpose of the study is to provide whatever information and insights may prove useful for the members and leaders of the Catholic pentecostal renewal. While I am greatly edified by what looks like authentic religiosity among the membership, and by the willing cooperation given by the leaders, I am not leading a promotional campaign for this religious movement. While I formulated a number of testable hypotheses based on sociological studies of other religious movements, I tried to come to the study with no strong preconceptions, either favorable or unfavorable.

We have probably reached a level of sophistication where we no longer doubt that the tools and methods of social science research can be applied to the study of religious groups. Whether or not a study of this kind has any utility for the religious movement under investigation seems to depend on the attitudes of the members themselves.[31] Is it simply "God's work," in which the human individual allows himself to be passively inspired and guided? Or is it a movement to which human energy and ingenuity must be brought, goals established, plans made, communication developed, and structures built? Despite protestations to the contrary, this is what is happening in the Catholic pentecostal movement.

2

The Paraclete Cult

Sociologists tend to categorize groups of people according to the structures they employ and the functions they perform. In researching religious groups and theorizing about them, they usually follow, and expand upon, the classic models discussed by Ernst Troeltsch, who found that the religious structures and functions of Christianity were exemplified simultaneously and historically in three main sociological types: the church, the sect, and mysticism.[1] Forty years ago Howard Becker rearranged this typology by inserting the denomination between *ecclesia* and sect, and by substituting the term "cult" for Troeltsch's mysticism.[2] American sociologists have tended to neglect the sociological implications of the religious cult and have done an almost inordinate amount of research on religious sects.

These four types of religious groups have often been discussed as though they were independent and separate entities and also, in popular evolutionary theory, as though there were sometimes a successive development from cult to sect to denomination to *ecclesia*.[3] I have argued elsewhere that all large-scale religious bodies (generally fitting the description of *ecclesia*) contain within themselves smaller groupings with characteristics that are cultic, sectlike, and denominational.[4] The findings of our research project on American Catholic pentecostals demonstrate quite clearly that the charismatic renewal is most appropriately called, in sociological terms, a religious cult that is both structurally and functionally contained within the larger Roman Catholic Church.

Cult and Sect

The concept of the existence of cult-within-*ecclesia* is not exceptional even among non-Christian religions. Anthropologists dealing with primitive societies describe the cult as one aspect, or segment, of the total religious system of the tribe or society under study. Thus, one reads of "ancestral cults" among the religions of China and Africa, and of the peyote cult and others among American Indians. In a similar way, rituals, liturgy, and worship services are a necessary ingredient of all religions in the Judaic-Christian tradition.

As defined by Catholic scriptural and theological scholars, the cult is an *anamnesis,* a "recalling to mind," or a "ceremonial representation of a salutary event of the past, in order that the event may lay hold of the situation of the celebrant." Strictly defined, the focus of the cult is God himself, and not a shrine, a statue, or a saint. As a religious ceremony, it is a service which is expressly offered to God in adoration, praise, thanksgiving, and petition, and which acknowledges God's supreme power.[5]

The people who participate in this ritual act of worship constitute the group recognized by sociologists as a cult. Their religious practices conform to Troeltsch's description of mysticism as "the insistence upon a direct inward and present religious experience. It takes for granted the objective forms of religious life in worship, ritual, myth, and dogma; and it is either a reaction against these objective practices, which it tries to draw back into the living process, or it is the supplementing of traditional forms of worship by means of a personal and living stimulus."[6]

The contemporary Americans who call themselves Catholic charismatics, or pentecostals, focus their devotion on the Paraclete, the Holy Spirit, the third divine person of the Trinity. They point out that this is not something original, or new, or unusual in the history of Catholicism. Cultic elements were present in the Catholic Church before sectarianism blossomed with the Reformation, and it is a commonplace for sociologists of religion to point out that the personal, spiritual, mystical, and "individualizing" tendencies of Catholicism were safely lodged in the monasteries.[7] Demerath and Hammond remark that "part of the genius of Catholicism has been its ability to make room for its dissidents by turning them into orders and restricting them to the sidelines."[8]

It is, of course, a major historical misinterpretation to suggest that the disciples of Benedict, Francis of Assisi, Dominic, Ignatius Loyola, and other founders of religious orders were relegated to the "sidelines." Perhaps they were "dissidents" in the fact that they sought a more satisfactory structure through which to serve God and His people. The Catholic pentecostal movement diverges from historical precedent in that its members, even though seeking a more satisfying way to worship God, have no intention of being shunted into monasteries or cloisters.

Religious sectarians, however, are dissidents who cut themselves off from the parent church and often express

21

"defiance of the world or withdrawal from it, a greater or lesser rejection of the legitimacy of the demands of the secular sphere."[9] This says nothing of the sect's devotional practices and theological beliefs, which in many instances may be quite similar to those of the religious cult. The sociological and structural significance lies in the sect's separatism, which emerges mainly from its opposition to the way in which the parent church accommodates to the secular society. The outstanding contemporary example of this phenomenon in American Catholicism is the so-called Boston Heresy Case of Leonard Feeney and his followers.[10]

The history of Christianity is sprinkled with descriptions of religious groups—from Montanists to Camisards and Moravians—who withdrew in protest from the larger Church, or were excommunicated from the parent body.[11] Sociological research on the varieties of sects has resulted in an extensive literature which highlights, particularly on the American scene, the splintering and proliferation of Protestant groups. The typological study of sects reveals large differences in structure, practice, doctrine, and goals. What they have in common is a dissatisfaction with the routinized traditions of the established churches and a readiness to follow their own separate ways to religious salvation.

The appearance of pentecostalism among Protestants at the turn of the century was the signal for further splintering into religious sects. In some instances these charismatics withdrew voluntarily from the parent denomination; in others they were virtually forced out. They were seen as a threat to the established doctrines and rituals of the mainline churches, and as they separated themselves from these churches, they evangelized, and thus proliferated rapidly.[12] This was especially true of the Assemblies of God. After the middle of the century the pentecostal revival touched members of the Episcopal Church, and they were warned in a pastoral letter from Bishop James Pike on May 2 1963 that their practice of tongue speaking was "heresy in embryo."

While there is some evidence of heterodox tendencies that suggest sectarianism among Catholic charismatics, there is much weightier evidence that Catholic pentecostalism represents personal cultic renewal within the organized Church. The pentecostals are a group of Roman Catholics who associate for the purpose of intensifying their own spiritual life and of sharing with others the ecstatic experience of the gifts of the Holy Spirit. While the focus of this religious cult is God, the Paraclete, one may recall Becker's earlier description of the goal of the membership as "that of purely personal ecstatic experience, salvation, comfort, and mental or physical healing."[13]

The New Pentecost

The religious cult of the Paraclete is sometimes identified as "Catholic pentecostalism," but the label preferred by the membership is "charismatic," which of course refers to the charisms of the Paraclete. These are the extraordinary graces, powers, or gifts granted to the individual Christian for the good of the Church. As Gelpi remarks, "the seven gifts of the Holy Spirit endow one with docility to the Spirit in acquiring the mind of Christ and in actively associating oneself with his messianic mission.[14] In concrete associational terms, Stephen Clark says, "the charismatic renewal is a set of practices (praying with people to be baptized in the Spirit, praying with them for healing, speaking in tongues and prophecy, spontaneous worship, etc.), and an informally structured type of meeting (the prayer meeting and the Day of Renewal)."[15]

The sociologist makes no judgment about theological

charisma as an endowment of divine grace. The concept came to the attention of social scientists mainly through the works of Max Weber, who used it to distinguish effectively between the prophetic and the priestly persons and functions in religious collectivities. "We shall understand 'prophet' to mean a purely individual bearer of charisma, who by virtue of his mission proclaims a religious doctrine or divine commandment. . . . The personal call is the decisive element distinguishing the prophet from the priestly class."[16]

Translating these concepts to the contemporary Catholic scene, we recognize Catholic pentecostals as prophetic, extraordinary, Spirit-filled people who are distinguishable from conventional Catholics. The latter keep to accepted religious practices and forms and make no claim to unusual and extraordinary gifts of the Spirit. They simply serve the sacred traditions of the church in a patterned and routine manner. In a sense they may be called "institutional" Christians, while the charismatics, who pledge loyalty to the institutional church, may at the same time be called "personalized" Christians.

It should be pointed out that while the sociological observer tends to label the Catholic pentecostal as "different," and his charisms as "extraordinary," this is not necessarily the view of the theological observer. Indeed, Hans Küng insists that "we misunderstand the charismata when we think of them mainly as extraordinary, miraculous and sensational phenomena."[17] They are not meant to be the possession of the specially chosen children of God. "They are rather altogether ordinary phenomena in the life of the Church" and are not limited to office-holders, like bishops and other hierarchs, nor to a separate class of Christians with sectarian tendencies.

In associating with one another, Catholic charismatics enact patterns of behavior that are exclusively religious. They do not constitute a secular social movement for purposes of economic, political, educational, or other institutional reform, either in the Catholic Church or in the American society. In some vague ways they think that church reform "ought" to come as a kind of spin-off from personal reform, and they are even more vague about the reform of the total socio-cultural system. These attitudes are difficult to interpret from a sociological point of view, yet we cannot completely by-pass the question of why this pentecostal religious cult became so popular among American Catholics in the late 1960's.

Catholic charismatics maintain that there is nothing "new" about the gifts of the Holy Spirit and that they have been manifest among Christians ever since the first Pentecost. Yet they are quite sure that the beginning of the pentecostal movement among Protestants can be dated on the eve of the new year, 1900, when Charles Parham and Agnes Ozman received Spirit baptism, and among Catholics, on a spiritual retreat in February 1967. "That was the Duquesne weekend that signalled the beginning of the charismatic renewal in the Roman Catholic Church."[18]

Sociologists tend increasingly to regard a cult as "a very loose organization characteristic of a rapidly secularizing society or one which is atomistic and disorganized."[19] There are many sociological and psychological theories which seek to explain the rise of religious movements: they may be seen as developing in response to structural strain, to social upheaval, or to economic, cultural, or spiritual deprivation, or they may be understood as a collective attempt to solve personal and social problems.[20] It is simplistic to exclude all these explanations on the grounds that God is at work

25

in the world and picks His own time to manifest the pentecostal charisma.

All of these theories are found in the literature on religious movements, but we may turn from them to an explanation suggested by Donald Gelpi, a leading spokesman for Catholic pentecostalism. "Catholics who have been 'baptized charismatically' in the Spirit may well be inclined to look upon the movement as God's response to the factionalism that has been growing in the American church."[21] He perceives this "factionalism" mainly in the increasing polarization between traditionalists and liberals "which resulted from the effort to implement the directives of Vatican II."

The implication of this suggestion is that the various reforms instituted in the name of Pope John's aggiornamento became a source of contention among Catholics and that this "social upheaval" within the Church disturbed these prayerful Catholics, who were moved by the Spirit to transcend such internal polarization. "The bitterest failure of the years of reform in the Church has been the evident failure of spiritual regeneration, which seems to have been Pope John's principal hope for the Council."[22] Indeed, Catholic pentecostals like to go back to the Pope's opening prayer, delivered to the council on Christmas day 1961: "May the Divine Spirit deign to answer in a most comforting manner the prayer that rises daily to Him from every corner of the earth: Renew Your wonders in our time, as though for a new Pentecost."[23]

The new Pentecost promises the renewal of the Church, and the renewal of the Church starts with the reform of the individual. This means that through a reinvigorated interior and spiritual life, the prevailing factionalism should disappear—or be substantially lessened—and that pentecostalism should be the effective force for Christian unity.

Internal antagonisms will subside; differences between liberals and conservatives will be unimportant; and dissidents will be brought together in peace and love within the one, holy, catholic, and apostolic Church.

Sectarianism

It would appear that a religious cult with aspirations of this kind could hardly be called sectarian (that is, with tendencies to split from the parent Catholic Church). As one respondent to our survey said: "The charismatic renewal could never thrive as a separate group. It must include all laymen and all clergy. I believe we are seeing this beginning already." The leadership of the movement warns the group members also against internal "separatism," that is, against a feeling of spiritual elitism by which they would consider themselves better than those Catholics who have not been baptized in the Spirit. Another respondent remarked, "Personally, I feel that the Lord is building up His church with the gifts of the Holy Spirit, which are meant for everybody, and not just for a select few."

Let us review the pertinent data from our national sample survey of lay Catholic charismatics to see whether, and to what extent, there are sectarian or separatist tendencies among them. We had suggested that one of the principal benefits coming from membership in the movement might be "a sense of freedom from institutional religion," but this was totally rejected by the respondents. With this attitude clearly established, we may look at three areas of potential withdrawal from the Church: (1) relations with the home parish; (2) attitudes toward the clergy; and (3) adherence to orthodox religious beliefs and practices.

(1) Although Catholic charismatics are seeking religious experiences that are not ordinarily provided in the conven-

tional Catholic parish, we do not find a significant number of them who have actually broken from their home parish. While the majority (68%) of them meet in prayer groups outside their own parish, nine out of ten (89%) attend weekly mass in their parish church. Six out of ten (61%) think that their home parish is "very much" or "somewhat" a genuine Christian community, and only one-fourth (24%) report that they are not now, nor have ever been, active in parish groups and societies. All of them continue to contribute money to their parish, and some (52%) give even more than they used to before becoming involved in the pentecostal movement.

Several pentecostal leaders who have reviewed these findings point out that they deliberately avoid holding charismatic eucharistic services on Saturdays and Sundays precisely because they do not want pastors to charge them with divisiveness. Thus, if the lay people are to fulfill their mass obligation, they have no choice except to go to the parish church. The leaders urge them to participate in parish activities, not simply to demonstrate solidarity with the local congregation, but also to infuse the ordinary parishioners with the spirit of charismatic renewal. There is a general feeling that many local parish priests are "suspicious" of the charismatic renewal and that they need to be "converted" by the prayers of the membership.

An exception to this generalization about close parochial ties seems to be developing in the so-called covenant communities promoted by some of the leaders who control the communications media of the movement. The covenant community, with its subcommunities and households, operates as an essentially extra-parochial structure. None of the 155 prayer groups we surveyed is organized along these lines, although the members of some of them have seriously discussed the advisability of entering into an exclusive covenant. Josephine Ford uses the examples of covenant communities at Ann Arbor and South Bend to demonstrate a structural development quite different from that of the large majority of charismatic prayer groups.[24]

(2) In spite of their prayerful attitude toward the local priests, there is no clear and wide manifestation of anti-clericalism among the charismatics, nor is there any tendency to separate themselves from the Catholic clergy and hierarchy. Eight out of ten (78%) affirm that Pope Paul VI is the infallible Vicar of Christ. Three-quarters of them are of the opinion that the charismatic movement could not continue in existence without the presence and aid of priests. More than half (55%) report that they have had the parish priest in their home during the past year. The same proportion would obey their bishop if he were to prohibit charismatic prayer meetings in his diocese.

The fact that a substantial minority would be unwilling to accept their bishop's prohibition points up a crucial problem for the renewal movement. Harold Cohen, who had seen these statistics before the 1973 International Conference, said in his keynote message, "We need to be obedient to Church authorities." He pledged obedience to the hierarchy and added that "I would drop every charismatic activity in New Orleans tomorrow if my bishop told me to." This statement gained a sharp rebuttal from Paul de Celles, a coordinator of the People of Praise Community, who objected to this "extraordinary public commitment of obedience." He said, "I take issue with the notion that we should automatically obey a bishop who asks us to stop participation in the Catholic charismatic renewal."[25]

Our research data reveal a small minority (14.6%) of "dissenters" who do not think that priests are necessary to the movement, and who also said they would not obey an order of the bishop to disband. Among these are a few well-trained lay leaders who, like de Celles, feel that there is in the movement "a trend toward a clericalism which does not reflect the Spirit-led attitude of thousands of people in the charismatic renewal." One of our informants detects a kind of "subtle clericalism" among some priest-leaders who are afraid of lay involvement in the teaching ministry of the movement.

(3) The question of orthodoxy in religious beliefs and practices elicits some mixed and ambivalent answers. It is true that some of the expressions of prayer and piety at the group meetings are not customary among the majority of Catholics, but they can hardly be termed unorthodox. At the level of belief everybody affirms the true presence of Christ in the eucharist, and everybody now reads the sacred scriptures more than ever before. The majority of respondents receive Holy Communion (77%), attend mass (76%), and visit the Blessed Sacrament (63%) more than they had previously done. Some also go to confession (37%) and recite the rosary (30%) more frequently since becoming active in the pentecostal movement.

. That there is another and unorthodox side to this matter is recognized by Edward O'Connor, who writes that "some Catholics seem surprisingly ready to abandon the doctrines and discipline of the Church when they encounter the Pentecostal experience."[26] Our research questionnaire did not reach lay charismatics who have abandoned the Catholic Church, although some of our respondents told us about such people. Among the current lay membership, however, we did find tendencies toward certain Protestant religious doctrines, with which we shall deal in another chapter.[27] One of the most serious of these is the so-called salvation experience attendant upon baptism in the Spirit. More than half (55%) of our respondents agree that "accepting Jesus as my personal Savior means that I am already saved."

Covenant Community

Despite some of the ambivalent tendencies exhibited by these lay Catholic charismatics, it seems correct to make the generalization that the great majority of them think of themselves as loyal members of the Church who have no intention of breaking off into a sectarian group. Although they are loosely organized and are not canonically structured within the diocesan system, they are not counter-ecclesial and are only vaguely anti-institutional. In a sense, they fit the description of what Herbert Blumer calls an "expressive movement," that is, one in which "the individual comes to terms with an unpleasant external reality by modifying his reactions to that reality, not by modifying the external reality itself."[28]

Up to this point we have used the term *reform* to refer only to the efforts of sectarian groups, that is, of people who have separated themselves from the Church with the intention of changing and purifying the religious system. We may talk of reform also as a process of adaptation, of making changes from within in the structures and institutions of the Church. John McEleney made a similar distinction in pointing out that renewal is not the same as reform, or adaptation. By renewal he meant an "interior renovation of the spirit by which the very essence of religious life, that is, the deeper association with and consecration of man to our suffering Redeemer, should be lived ever more profoundly."[29]

Although this explanation was directed toward the religious orders of the Church, it also defines the central purpose of the Paraclete cult—the purpose that causes us to identify it sociologically as an internal religious cult of renewal rather than an external sectarian movement of reform. The leaders and members of the pentecostal groups would certainly agree with the Fathers of Vatican II, who proclaimed that "even the most desirable changes made on behalf of contemporary needs will fail of their purpose unless a renewal of spirit gives life to them. Indeed such an interior renewal must always be accorded the leading role even in the promotion of exterior works."[30]

The personal regenerative aspect of charismatic renewal forms a continuing theme in the comments that participants added to the survey questionnaire. A typical remark is that "since becoming a member of this movement my life has changed in such a way that somehow is hard to explain. My spiritual life has taken on much more meaning. It is a joy to go to Mass. My daily life is being lived for God in everything I do. I have turned myself over to Him completely. Praise the Lord!" Essentially the same kind of fervent testimony is given by the great majority of members, centering almost always on what God has done for the individual. Similar declarations are made when members give witness at the prayer meetings. The movement's monthly periodical, *New Covenant,* is also characterized by personal and subjective revelations of the conversion experience. The so-called charismatic experience is described as a deeply spiritual, psychological, and sometimes emotional, phenomenon.

Although there is great emphasis on personal expressions of individualistic piety, which manifest a joyful relationship with the Paraclete, there is also much talk of "sharing" and much writing about "community" among the members of the cult. Their group behavior at meetings is in direct contrast to the relatively aloof and formalistic relations that Catholics normally exhibit in the Church congregation at

Mass. They show marked affection for one another, embracing and kissing, using Christian names, and generally behaving in the familiar fashion of the primary face-to-face group. There is a sense of concern and fellowship that is again markedly different from that which exists among the members of the typical Catholic parish. As Harrison remarks, they are striving to "substitute deeper relationships for the anonymity of the conventional parish."[31]

This manifestation of intimate primary relations does not belie the "individualizing tendencies" of pentecostal piety, nor does it bespeak a lack of concern for the reformation of the Church. One may say that there is a desire to "pentecostalize" the Church and to Christianize the society, but the latter is expressed in their oft-repeated slogan, "to build a new society within the shell of the old." What they are talking about is the expansion of the local prayer group into a covenant community, which is neither a new kind of parish nor a new kind of religious order. It remains snugly and loyally within the bosom of Mother Church, but it withdraws from secular society, which is corrupt and incorrigible.

One of the chief pentecostal spokesmen, Stephen Clark, explains the need for this withdrawal from the sordid world. "When society as a whole cannot be expected to accept Christianity, then it is necessary to form communities within society to make Christian life possible."[32] The leaders make much of Karl Rahner's baleful vision of Christians as now being or soon to be a diaspora—dispersed individuals and groups practicing the faith in an otherwise secularized, if not paganized, world. Michael Harrison, who made a study of Clark's Ann Arbor prayer community, remarks that "the Pentecostal movement within the Church provided an alternative for people who could not find spiritual fulfillment in the new secularity."

Instead of trying to change the world, or to "modify

33

the unpleasant external reality," as Blumer says, the charismatic covenant community retains the definition of the typical religious cult: "A collectivity that has the continuity of a social movement but that makes demands only on the behavior of its members. A religious cult may demand behavior of its members that is quite different from the established social conventions, while making no effort to promote acceptance of such a program by the society."[33] This is an important distinction because the charismatic community insists that it is not task-oriented. It does not use a "functional" approach, but bases its solidarity, under God, on the human relations and values of the committed members. "Its members do not work together as a community to produce something or to effect a change in society."[34]

Levels of Organization

It must be noted that the covenant community is an exceptional phenomenon in the Catholic pentecostal movement. The overwhelming majority of American charismatic prayer groups have not developed into covenant communities and probably never will. The covenant community is exceptional also in that only totally committed persons, the spiritual elite who are willing to share common meals and prayer and even households, make up the community. In other words, while it is theoretically for everybody in the movement, it is practically limited to relatively few.

In sociological terms the cult of the Paraclete has now become a large religious movement, or organization, that has its roots in the local community but extends as a social network over the whole country. The leading spokesmen do not like to call it an association, or organization, or federation, or even a movement. They dislike structures and institutions, and insist that the work of the Spirit must not be routinized in the lives of the people. In fact, however, all of this has happened and is happening in the charismatic renewal.

Like most religious cults and sects at their inception, the original charismatic groups wanted to be free and spontaneous. There was no thought of structures, program planning, elective or appointive offices, leadership, or authority. As the membership increased and the groups multiplied around the country, this original concept changed, as it had to. Within two years of the famous retreat weekend at Duquesne, there was a cultic organization with programs to plan and with people "in charge." There had sprung up "a representative group of mature leaders from around the country." The formal bureaucracy began with the formation of a Service Committee of two priests and five laymen, "people who had been accepted as national leaders in the charismatic renewal." During the course of the year, an Advisory Committee was formed which included several Canadians; its membership comprised thirteen priests, ten laymen, two sisters, and one brother.[35]

There is still an odd, almost unreal, reluctance to admit that the spontaneous cult of the Paraclete has become a structured organization. Because it is a spiritual renewal, "an unorganized movement, there can be no authority structure within it. The only authority can be the authority that comes from services well performed." It is true, of course, that one of the principal functions of all persons in authority in any type of organization is to be of service to its constituents.[36] It is a published fact that the authority of the charismatic leaders was exercised to exclude Professor J. Massingberd Ford from the conference because of her "disruptive and divisive behavior."[37]

Given the originating impetus of the Holy Spirit and the

continuing charisms of the membership, there are certain necessary this-worldly requirements for the spread of a social movement, and the cult of the Paraclete possesses all of them. These specific requirements are: (*a*) leadership, (*b*) an ideology, (*c*) a program, (*d*) communication, and (*e*) a favorable public image. At the national level one need only be a constant reader of *New Covenant* to recognize that all of these sociological elements are present in the Catholic pentecostal movement.

At the local or parochial level there are still many prayer groups that remain relatively autonomous and loosely organized. In those areas, however, where the movement is flourishing, like New Orleans, San Francisco, Ann Arbor, South Bend, and Rutherford, all of these functional prerequisites are clearly in evidence. Local leaders form the pastoral team under whose benign supervision the various service teams and ministries operate. A high level sub-unit is the core community, which is made up of the more faithful and enthusiastic members and promotes Life-in-the-Spirit and Growth-in-the-Spirit seminars. The regular weekly prayer meetings are augmented by the monthly Day of Renewal and the occasional diocesan, statewide, or regional conference.

The ideology of the Paraclete cult is communicated and reinforced not only by printed literature and a growing volume of tape cassettes, but also by prominent national charismatic leaders who travel about the country on an irregular schedule of lecture tours. It is the function of every member to mold and uphold the public image of the renewal movement, but it is especially the leaders who are sensitive to criticism from two general sources. One criticism commonly voiced by conventional clergy and laity is that the cult attracts psychologically aberrant personalities. The other criticism, usually made by concerned prelates, is that the movement is operating outside the canonical and ecclesiastical structures of Catholicism, building "a church within the Church," and this observation parallels that of the charismatics who see the movement as building a "new society within the shell of the old."[38]

Whither Now?

The social scientist is usually chary about "plotting trends" and even more so about predicting the future of volatile religious movements like the Paraclete cult. We have seen how the Catholic charismatic renewal—reluctantly and almost in spite of itself—has become large, complex, and structured. It has deliberately become more involved with pentecostals in the main-line Protestant churches. It has been exported to foreign countries and has developed international charismatic relations. If the power and influence of the Holy Spirit is infinite, there can be no end in sight. If the renewal is His work, as the members insist, human beings dare not put limitations upon it.

The sociologist sees the movement as an unexpected development within American Catholicism, but there are those, like the fifty-six-year-old New Yorker, who say: "It's nothing really new. The Holy Spirit movement is primarily a revival of what is a traditional part of Catholic doctrine, the doctrine of the indwelling of the Holy Spirit." The theologians of the movement are at pains to trace charismatic manifestations back through the centuries to the original Pentecost. This notion, that pentecostalism was "always there" in the Catholic Church, is accompanied now by a kind of prophecy that the movement itself will vanish as a sociological phenomenon.

According to this view there *is* an end in sight. The contemporary charismatic movement is seen as a type of spiritual force for church renewal that will lose its identity as it becomes fully absorbed into the whole of Catholicism. No less a personage than Cardinal Suenens has predicted that Catholic pentecostalism "will disappear as a movement as quickly as possible and enter into the blood and life of the Church. Once the river gets to the sea you don't speak of the river any more."[39] George Martin points out that "the goal is a charismatically renewed Church, not a separate pentecostal organization for people who go for that sort of thing."[40] Such spokesmen suggest parallels with the once flourishing biblical and liturgical movements which are no longer structurally identifiable within the Catholic Church because their purposes have been accomplished. The day of the biblical "pioneer" and the liturgical "crusader" is over, and these movements have vanished.

It does not behoove the social scientist to indulge in forecasting, but it is possible to point out dissimilarities between the organized cult of the Paraclete on the one hand and the professional associations of scholars and other experts that sponsored liturgical reform and biblical studies on the other. These "movements" never had induction ceremonies, grass-roots membership, prayer households, differential service roles, levels of leadership and authority, or a programed and innovative style of life. Unlike the Paraclete cult, they were not institutionalized and organized religious movements, and they did not command personal commitment.

The Catholic pentecostal movement may fade in popularity, lose membership, and become disorganized, as has happened to some religious congregations, but in sociological terms this represents the death of failure rather than absorption into the "blood and life" of the Church.

3

Heterodoxy in Charismatic Renewal

The founding fathers of the contemporary charismatic renewal among American Catholics gratefully reveal their spiritual indebtedness to Protestant pentecostals. As Robert Frost, a prominent pentecostal minister, recently said, "In the beginning you Catholics had a lot to learn from us, the classical and neo-Pentecostals, and you did."[1] The early leaders of the Catholic movement at Duquesne and Notre Dame Universities attended Protestant pentecostal prayer meetings and invited pentecostal ministers to speak to their groups. One of the leaders, Kevin Ranaghan, recalls that "we depended heavily not only on the friendship and prayer, but also on the encouragement, pastoral guidance, and seasoned experience of Protestant pentecostals."[2]

It is also now part of the brief history of Catholic pentecostalism that inspiration and encouragement have come to the membership from a best-selling book by a Protestant minister, David Wilkerson, called *The Cross and the Switchblade*. Almost as important has been John Sherrill's *They*

Speak with Other Tongues. In many places these books have become "must" reading for members of the Catholic charismatic movement, and they are used almost like introductory textbooks to attract prospective members to the renewal movement.[3] Collateral introductory reading includes the first three chapters of the *Acts of the Apostles*, but one gets the impression that these are a kind of backup for Wilkerson's and Sherrill's evidence that the Holy Spirit is at work in the modern world.

Catholic pentecostals continue to have frequent contact with Protestant pentecostals, not only as a demonstration of ecumenical fellowship and mutual support, but also as a persisting and shared learning situation. The pages of *New Covenant* are open to Protestant ministers like Brick Bradford, Graham Pulkingham, Vinson Synan, J. Rodman Williams, and others, and this periodical no longer calls itself the magazine of the Catholic Charismatic Renewal. The annual charismatic conference at Notre Dame University includes in its program some of the leading spokesmen for Protestant pentecostalism.

This openness to Protestantism frightens Archbishop Dwyer who publicly denounced the 1974 International Conference at Notre Dame University and gave a scathing criticism of the charismatic renewal. "We regard it bluntly as one of the most dangerous trends in the Church in our time, closely allied in spirit with other disruptive and divisive movements; threatening grave harm to her unity and damage to countless souls." Catholic prelates may worry about the Protestant influence on their people, about their "being misled and not being firmly grounded in sound theology"[4]— but it was a Protestant clergyman, David du Plessis, who issued the friendly warning at the 1969 conference that Catholics should not "imitate uncritically the beliefs and practices of Protestant Pentecostal groups."[5] It is the intent of this chapter to investigate whether or not Catholic lay charismatics have heeded Dr. du Plessis's counsel.

Pentecostal Influence

Pentecostalism, in its Protestant and classical form, is one segment of the energetic and fast-growing "third force" that is competing with main-line Protestantism and Catholicism for the salvation of mankind in Christendom.[6] The wide variety of labels adopted by these so-called fringe sects — adventist, holiness, evangelical, conservative, and fundamentalist—can by no means be employed synonymously. For example, pentecostal groups are anathema to Carl McIntire's neo-fundamentalist American Council of Christian Churches, and Pat Boone was excommunicated from the Church of Christ when he became a pentecostal. Further, there are doctrinal and structural variations among the religious groups that call themselves pentecostals. Many religious sects claim this title, but most of them are affiliated with the Pentecostal Fellowship of North America, and the largest groups are the Assemblies of God, the Church of God in Christ, and the United Pentecostal Church. Thus, Synan could make the boast that "already there are more Pentecostals in the world than there are Methodists or Baptists."[7]

The most noticeable influence of Protestant pentecostalism is in the external patterns of group prayer and devotional piety now exhibited by Catholic charismatics. The conventional Catholic, familiar with the Mass and Benediction, novenas and rosaries, encounters new and strange practices at his first charismatic prayer meeting: people raising their arms in prayer, clapping hands while singing hymns,[8] giving testimony to their personal religious experiences, spontaneously reading a passage from scripture or proclaiming a prophecy, murmuring ejaculations of praise and thanks to the Lord, and above all, speaking and singing in tongues. These are behavioral oddities that are certainly not "the thing to do" at Catholic worship services—and had not been "done" until introduced by the pentecostals.[9]

There are other "new"—and even more spectacular— customs. The adherents of Protestant pentecostalism are essentially pneumatocentric; they generally manifest the charismata of the Holy Spirit in such activities as faith healing, glossolalia, prophecy, exorcism, and, especially, the baptism of the Spirit. Only recently have these practices been "taken over," as it were, by Catholics involved in the charismatic renewal movement. There is nothing obviously and theologically unorthodox about them. As Donald Gelpi writes, "The charismatic gifts, like the gift of tongues, of prophecy, of mystical and visionary experience, and the power of healing and exorcism, are vital, visible signs to the eucharistic community of the life its members share through the activity of the Spirit of Christ."[10]

In our national survey of lay Catholic members of the renewal movement, we found that, apart from such authentic, if unconventional, mannerisms, there are manifestations of seriously unorthodox religious doctrines among some of the Catholic prayer groups. One member from western New York reported that "pressure" was being brought on his group to accept such non-Catholic teachings as rebaptism by immersion, demon-chasing, nondenominationalism, rejection of the hierarchical priesthood, and personal and exclusive reliance on the Scriptures. Some are being told that devotion to Mary and the saints is idolatry and that traditional Catholic doctrine is in error. A highly educated member who had been a religious sister detects in her prayer group "the heresy that the Holy Spirit is a separate and most powerful God."

It is a fact that some charismatics, including priests and religious brothers and sisters, have embraced these teachings and abandoned the Catholic Church to join Assemblies of God and other pentecostal groups.[11] There are no statistical studies on Catholics who have left their Church as a consequence of the charismatic experience, nor, on the other hand, is there statistical information on the number of those who have been greatly strengthened in the Catholic faith as a result of this experience. We are on more certain ground when we analyze the replies of the 744 Catholic charismatics who took part in our national survey. Here we find that some members do accept certain heterodox doctrines, apparently under the illusion that these are orthodox beliefs of the Catholic Church.

Three Heterodox Teachings

Protestant pentecostalism got its start at a time when modernism was being attacked by official Catholic theologians and the Social Gospel movement was flourishing within the main-line Protestant denominations. It was also at the time when conservative and evangelical fundamentalists were beginning their attempts to eliminate "heresy" from such established denominations as the Disciples, Methodists, and Presbyterians.[12] We must leave it to Catholic theologians and Church historians to decide whether or not there are any parallels here to the relatively unexpected emergence of the contemporary pentecostal movement among Catholics. Ours is the much more modest task of examining the replies of Catholic lay charismatics in an effort to determine

43

whether or not they may have accepted certain common Protestant doctrines that are heterodox to the Catholic belief system.

In the questionnaire we prepared for our national survey, we requested affirmative or negative responses to a number of creedal positions in order to learn something about the religious belief system which the members profess. Among these were three statements which we would normally expect Catholic people to reject, but the results were otherwise: seven out of ten (71%) of the respondents agreed that "the Second Coming of Christ is imminent"; more than half (55%) affirmed that "accepting Jesus as my personal Savior means that I am already saved"; and half (51%) were willing to say that "the Spirit speaks to the heart—not the mind."

Many Protestant fringe sects are preoccupied with the idea that we are now in the "last days" and that the contemporary outpouring of the Holy Spirit is God's "final move in preparing a holy people for the Second Coming of Christ and to warn the world of the closing of the age."[13] In some of the religious groups there are overtones of messianism, chiliasm, or millenarianism, doctrines which have been repopularized in Hal Lindsey's best seller, *The Late Great Planet Earth*. Lindsey ends his book with the word, "maranatha," which means "the Lord is coming soon."[14] The assumption is that Christ will usher in, on his return, a long golden age of peace, happiness, and holiness.

Belief in the Second Coming is not alien to Catholics, who proclaim during the Mass "Lord Jesus, come in glory" and "Christ will come again." This belief is quite different, however, from that of the Adventists and other sectarians who hold that Christ's return will happen soon. Catholics generally do not believe that the Second Coming is imminent, and most of them probably share the attitude of one respondent, an attorney, who remarked, "I have no privileged information on this." Another, a lawyer from Maine, said, "This is ridiculous. If Jesus didn't tell His Apostles, how should I know?" Among charismatic Catholics, however, belief in an imminent Second Coming is a strongly held teaching.

The Protestant pentecostals' acceptance of the imminence of the Second Coming has obviously been "taken over" by these lay Catholics. If they read their magazine, *New Covenant,* carefully, they could receive the impression, if not the conviction, that the return of the Lord is to be expected in the near future. In a special issue on this subject, Phil O'Mara wrote that "it is quite possible that the time fixed by the Father is close at hand and that in a few months or years, or perhaps after one generation, the world will end." He reviews the apocalyptic literature, depicts the crises of our times, and concludes that "we need an eschatalogical faith, we need priorities founded on the conviction that Jesus is coming soon."[15]

This teaching is clearly widespread among the membership and it is taken seriously. A female accountant from Pennsylvania wrote, "I have come to believe that Jesus will soon return." Another respondent, a college professor, said he would not agree that "it will be a Jehovah Witness Spectacle, but agree that it is imminent." It should be noted, however, that one of the foremost theologians of the movement, Donald Gelpi, holds a different view: "The charismatic experience yields no certitude concerning the time of the second coming."[16]

The second heterodox teaching, to which more than half of the Catholic charismatics adhere, is the certainty of salvation—a doctrine strange to orthodox Catholic ears and one which was repudiated by the Council of Trent. John Wesley's doctrine of "entire sanctification" is the eager answer of the fundamentalist to the question "Have you been saved?" In this teaching the certainty of salvation emerges from a "work of grace wrought instantaneously in the heart of believers, upon consecration and faith, by the baptism of the Holy Spirit."[17] Orthodox Catholics accept Jesus as their savior, but they realize that eternal salvation cannot be guaranteed unconditionally on the basis of this acceptance.

One of the leading thinkers of the charismatic renewal movement, Prof. J. Massingberd Ford, warns: "We can never be certain of our salvation, and herein we differ from many non-Roman Catholic Christians: Never until we reach heaven can we be certain that we are saved. St. John says that the truth is not in him who says that he has no sin. Therefore, we must work out our salvation with fear and trembling, as scripture says."[18] Despite this warning, one can understand how the joyful uplift and emotional thrill felt by many charismatics when they receive Spirit baptism might be interpreted as a "salvation experience." Among the benefits they report having received from the charismatic experience, many of them rank high "a genuine conviction of my personal salvation."

The third heterodox notion, that the Spirit speaks to the heart rather than to the mind, is accepted by half the respondents to our survey. In a profound sense this questionnaire item was intended to test the balance between the intellectual and the emotional aspects of Catholic pentecostalism. It is a well-known fact that many fundamentalist preachers among the lower-class religious sects distrust theological learning. They are anti-intellectual and they are afraid that the theologizing of their religious experiences would lead to the pitfall of liberalism and worldliness. They depend upon their subjective feelings to guide them on the path to God.

The properly instructed Catholic would deny this survey statement and would probably agree with the engineer from Michigan who said, "The Spirit speaks to my heart through the charismatic experience, but also to my mind through scripture, teachers, prophecy and creation itself." Some Church authorities have worried that this healthy balance of heart and mind might be upset by pentecostal emotionalism. Bishop Jorge Martinez of Mexico City "criticized tendencies toward illuminism, anti-intellectualism, and irrationalism in the renewal and the importance that many people attach to extraordinary manifestations. He cautioned the faithful against excessive Protestant influence in the movement."[19]

One need only witness the emotional enthusiasm shown by many Catholic pentecostals at their prayer meetings to come to the suspicion that the subjective experience of the "heart" is more important to them than a balanced theological understanding of the religion they profess. The person who demonstrates the most enthusiasm is often considered the member who is most "Spirit-filled," and in some cases he or she is accepted as the normative leader of the local prayer group. Some of these people are probably suffering from the affliction that O'Connor calls "charismania."[20] While it is perhaps unfair to call them antinomian, thus implying that they believe that faith alone is necessary to salvation, one does not expect well-instructed Catholics to place such heavy emphasis on subjective piety.

From Heterodox to Orthodox

We have seen that there were proportional differences in the respondents' acceptance of these three key statements, and this means that the heterodox label cannot be applied to all of the lay Catholic pentecostals who answered the questionnaire. In order to make comparisons according to differences of response, we developed four statistical categories. Those we place in the heterodox category are the 215 persons (29%) who agree to all three statements: that the Second Coming is imminent; that they are already saved; and that the Spirit speaks only to the heart. At the opposite pole are the 100 orthodox people (13%) who disagree with all three statements. In between these two groups are the 243 pro-heterodox (33%), who accept two of the statements, and the 186 pro-orthodox (25%), who accept only one of them.

Table 3.1 explores some of the general background characteristics of the respondents in an attempt to discover explanatory elements. There are some small statistical differences showing that males, younger persons, and born Catholics tend to be slightly more orthodox than females, older persons, and converted Catholics. Larger differences show up, however, in the comparisons by education and occupational status. Older people of lower occupation and less Catholic schooling tend toward heterodoxy. What may be of more significance, and of more concern to the charismatic leadership of the country, is the heterodox tendency of lay charismatics in the Midwest. This region is the heartland of the charismatic renewal, and from it emanate the instructional books, pamphlets, articles, cassettes, and various other "services" that are meant to give guidance to the national membership. Yet this area has the highest proportion (67%) of lay charismatics who lean toward unorthodox doctrinal positions, while the East has the lowest proportion (55%).

Of all these factors the most influential appears to be the amount and kind of schooling that Catholic pentecostals have had. The willingness to accept Protestant religious

TABLE 3.1

Percentage Distribution of Four Categories of Catholic Pentecostals According to Selected Characteristics

	% Hetero dox	% Pro- hetero dox	% Pro- ortho- dox	% Ortho- dox	n
Sex					
Male	29	31	24	16	(375)
Female	29	34	26	11	(369)
Age					
Under 35 years	24	36	25	15	(232)
35 to 49 years	31	32	23	14	(367)
50 years and over	32	29	31	8	(145)
Born and Convert Catholics					
Born Catholic	29	32	25	14	(642)
Convert Catholic	28	38	26	8	(102)
Catholic Education					
Catholic elementary	27	33	24	16	(448)
Catholic high school	26	31	25	18	(333)
Catholic college	16	31	27	26	(197)
Occupation					
Professional-Managerial	20	31	30	19	(291)
White collar	33	32	23	12	(211)
Blue collar	36	34	22	8	(216)
Region					
East	29	26	28	17	(249)
Midwest	31	36	22	11	(270)
South	26	36	26	12	(148)
Far West	29	32	25	14	(77)
All Respondents	29	33	25	13	(744)

teaching seems to derive from a lack of knowledge of Catholic doctrine as taught in the colleges, high schools, and elementary schools of the Church. The general principle is demonstrated: the less schooling a person has, the more likely he is to accept heterodox doctrine. As Table 3.2 shows, the orthodox, who reject these teachings, are twice as likely (58%) as the heterodox (28%) to have graduated from college. An even more compelling explanation resides in the kind of schooling they had. Four out of ten (39%) of the orthodox, as compared to only 6% of the heterodox, graduated from Catholic colleges.

TABLE 3.2

Educational Experiences of the Four Categories of Catholic Pentecostals

	% Hetero- dox (n = 215)	% Pro- hetero- dox (n = 243)	% Pro- ortho- dox (n = 196)	% Ortho- dox (n = 100)
College graduates	28	37	41	58
Four years Catholic college	6	14	14	39
Four years Catholic high school	30	34	36	54
Eight years Catholic elementary	37	42	43	61

The research data in Table 3.2 are a confirmation of the concern for solid teaching repeatedly expressed by some of the priest-leaders of the charismatic movement. This concern is felt also by some of the rank-and-file membership. A registered nurse from Colorado who is among the ortho-

50

dox pentecostals writes: "One of my main concerns is the need for more teachings. I wish there was a team of charismatic priests and theologians traveling about the country to speak in the Catholic churches and visit our individual prayer meetings." Donald Gelpi agrees that local prayer groups should be provided with sound theological instruction. He adds that "there have been repeated pleas from those involved in the Catholic charismatic renewal for solid theological and pastoral guidance. But there are, I believe, indications that at the present time guidance is insufficient and sometimes theologically questionable, or even misleading."[21]

As the movement becomes more organized and formalized, it is also developing a teaching ministry to fill this need. The movement's monthly periodical, *New Covenant,* is instructional as well as informational. The Charismatic Renewal Services at Notre Dame advertise and distribute cassettes, pamphlets, and books. National leaders like Fathers Cohen, Kosicki, and MacNutt frequently address diocesan and regional conferences. The larger prayer communities have formal programs for Life-in-the-Spirit seminars and Growth-in-the-Spirit seminars.[22] The "teaching ministry" at the local level provides instruction in the form of homilies, scriptural exegeses, and other explanatory talks and lectures.

It appears from our survey, however, that this rapidly expanding organization is not adequately meeting the need for a teaching ministry of persons well versed in Catholic theology. That which the members have not learned in earlier schooling must be provided them by experts in doctrinal orthodoxy. The high incidence of people with heterodox tendencies suggests that the movement suffers from a shortage of properly trained teachers. As O'Connor points out, "If error sometimes finds its way into Pentecostal groups, this is largely due to the fact that it has encountered a doctrinal vacuum. Contemporary experience is making it clear that the lack of sound, deep and full instruction is one of the greatest and most dangerous weaknesses of American Catholicism today."[23] It is probably not an overstatement to observe that continuing contact with, and reliance on, Protestant pentecostalism is filling this "doctrinal vacuum" and is providing the "theologically questionable and misleading" guidance that Gelpi notes.

The Church and Change

There is no inherent reason why pentecostalism, whether of the Protestant or Catholic variety, should include tendencies to social conservatism. Earlier pentecostal movements among the Protestants attracted large numbers of relatively poorly educated people from the lower economic classes who tended to be both theologically and socially conservative. The lay Catholic charismatics in this survey are mainly middle-class in education, occupation, and income. We deliberately chose to label those who appear to be most influenced by Protestant pentecostalism "heterodox" rather than "fundamentalist." Nevertheless, we may recall that "Protestant fundamentalism in the twentieth century was a movement which came to be characterized by anti-intellectualism, other-worldliness, and separation—from the rest of Christendom and the American culture at large."[24]

There can be no doubt that Catholic pentecostals are in favor of change; they are participating in a religious revival; they are experiencing a personal "great awakening." Catholic pentecostals like to call the charismatic movement a renewal of the human spirit under the influence of the Holy Spirit. It is not clear that their understanding of spiritual renewal implies an acceptance of modernization, adaptation, and aggiornamento. Among some of them, especially those who are here called heterodox, the ideal seems to be to return to the early apostolic community. Their preoccupation with the contents of the Acts of the Apostles goes beyond the personal consequences of the historical Pentecost. Those who are the most heterodox are also those who are least willing to involve the Church in progressive social change.

For example, one of the "signs of the times" in the adaptive American culture is the growing demand for equal rights and opportunities for women. Nevertheless, the constitutional amendment banning discrimination against women because of their sex, which was passed by the U.S. Senate in March 1972, has not been welcomed by the American hierarchy and has been publicly attacked by conservative Catholics.[25] This generally negative attitude is reflected by the Catholic pentecostals who responded to this survey. Only three out of ten (29%) agree that "the Church should

TABLE 3.3

Percentage of Approval of Selected Proposals among Four Categories of Catholic Pentecostals

	% Hetro-dox	% Pro-hetero-dox	% Pro-ortho-dox	% Ortho-dox
Church should support Women's Liberation	21	29	32	39
Church should ordain women	32	30	38	40
Priests should have place on picket lines	44	59	63	71
Church should lead protest movements	46	51	59	71

53

support Women's Liberation." Those with heterodox tendencies were even lower in support (21%), while the orthodox category was higher (39%) than the average.

Some of the respondents confuse "Women's Liberation" with the various subgroups operating under that title. A public-relations man from Michigan who is in the pro-heterodox category says that "the Church should not involve itself with all the 'lib' nonsense being ballyhooed for fun and profit of the girls." A young married woman from Iowa objects that "the women's liberation movement fosters resentment, and the Church must not encourage bitterness. Abortion reform is one of their main goals and Catholics certainly cannot support that." A heterodox male from West Virginia feels that "women's liberation appears to be a lower-class movement, with working-class girls interested mainly in removing their bras. I disagree with them."

The confusion between the issue of equal rights for women and the excesses of some women's liberation groups did not extend to the survey question: "Do you favor the ordination of women to the priesthood?" The great majority of lay pentecostals answer this query negatively—only one-third (34%) approve of ordination for women. Here again we find the orthodox category (40%) more likely than the others to favor this change. A female schoolteacher from Connecticut remarks: "I could envision many problems with women as priests. But I do know two women who are ministers and they are great, Kathryn Kuhlman and Agnes Sanford." A salesman from Georgia favors the ordination of women to the diaconate, but "the scriptures seem to be against women priests and the theologians used to say it was impossible."

The unwillingness to change either in the general direction of women's rights or in the specific direction of ordination of women seems to be reflected in one of the "teachings" of the charismatic renewal—the approval of the notion that wives should submit to the authority of their husbands. Larry Christenson writes that "the wife will find the same joy in submitting to her husband as Christ does in submitting to the Father." He speaks of the realization "that order in family life, especially the headship of the man and the submission of the woman, is a work of God that takes place in our families."[26]

The trend of the modern family is away from patriarchy, and it is not likely that theological and scriptural arguments will noticeably affect that trend among American Catholic families. "More and more it becomes clear that it has been the practice of patriarchy rather than a developed Christian theology which has enthroned the husband as 'head.'" In the same vein Sidney Callahan writes, "Hopefully, Christianity will see our Western manifestation of the patriarchal society wither away just as transmuted and secularized Christian values obviated slavery and the rigid feudal caste system."[27] This, however, is not the attitude of the charismatic woman who reported that family relations improved after she submitted to the headship of her husband.[28]

Let us look briefly at two other survey items in Table 3.3 in which the difference of opinion between heterodox and orthodox is much more significant. On the questions of whether the Church should take the lead in social protest movements and whether it is proper for a priest to walk a picket line, there is a very large difference of twenty-five percentage points between the two groups. This unwillingness to look upon the Church and its clergy as agencies of social change may be the strongest of all demonstrations of conservative social attitudes. After all, the Protestant pentecostals were among the vigorous opponents of the Social Gospel movement at the beginning of this century.[29]

On the other hand, the charismatic Catholic in the orthodox category is likely to think of the organized Church as a participant in the effort to bring about desired improvements in the broader society. The likelihood becomes even greater if he or she is aware of the papal social encyclicals. It must be pointed out that the difference between the two categories does not lie in their social attitudes. Both groups are broadly in favor of social and cultural progress, but the orthodox thinks the Church should have a hand in it, while the heterodox thinks someone else should do it.

The conclusions drawn from these research data stand or fall on the three normative heterodox statements concerning the imminence of the Second Coming, the certitude of salvation, and the non-intellectual nature of communication from the Holy Spirit. Several charismatic leaders to whom I have shown these findings protest that "they didn't mean it that way." The objective social scientist has to accept what people say; he must leave it to the psychologist to interpret the meaning of their statements, and to the theologian to explain what they ought to believe and how they ought to say it.

A supporter of the charismatic renewal may rejoice that only three in ten (29%) of the members exhibit strong heterodox tendencies, or he may grieve that only a relatively small percentage (13%) are completely free of such doctrinal aberrations. In discussing this matter Edward O'Connor writes that the original Pentecostals deserved to be called fundamentalist, but that "this was not because they were Pentecostal, but because of the fact that most of them were people of little education, incapable of distinguishing between scholarly interpretation and sophistic falsification." He assures us, however, that in the Catholic Church "this fundamentalist trait has not reappeared, except in a few groups that have been strongly influenced by the main-line Pentecostals."[30]

56

In summary, then, the findings of this survey demonstrate that David du Plessis's caution against imitating Protestant pentecostalism has not been widely heeded. There is a continuing imitation of devotional mannerisms, prayer practices, and other customs that have unquestionably energized the personal spirituality of Catholic charismatics. More seriously, however, there is a marked tendency among the lay members toward accepting certain heterodox teachings from the Protestant pentecostals, and this fact is reflective of an inadequate and poorly prepared teaching ministry within the charismatic movement. This doctrinal heterodoxy is accompanied also by a reluctance to see the Catholic Church take the lead in social aggiornamento.

4

The Changing Membership

The brief history of the contemporary charismatic renewal has been a success story in terms of rapid expansion. Prayer groups have multiplied all over the country, and more are being established in foreign countries. From its small American beginnings in the Midwest, Catholic pentecostalism has gone international. The *Directory* of member groups is out of date almost as soon as it is published. The annual summer conference on the campus of Notre Dame University taxes the surrounding housing facilities by attracting larger crowds every year. No pentecostal leader takes credit for the fact that "the Church, on every level, is becoming increasingly open to the work of the Holy Spirit. It is God himself who is doing this."[1]

Divine success, however, is sometimes countered by human failure. Groups fall apart and members drop out. Bert Ghezzi confesses that "despite its widespread success, the charismatic renewal is not without its failures. Among these are prayer groups which do not survive. Often, groups experience charismatic wildfire but later fold up."[2] He then explains how to put into effect the "considerable corporate wisdom" that the Lord has given the charismatic movement. Four essential elements can be assured by the hard work of the Catholic pentecostals. They are: operative prayer meetings, responsible pastoral care, effective initiation of new members, and basic teaching for all members. This human effort, of course, is always expended in cooperation "with the Lord."

The membership shifts as individuals come and go. One of the first persons interviewed for this study said that she benefited tremendously from regular attendance at weekly prayer meetings over a period of two years, but now attends only occasionally because she "no longer feels the need" for this group experience. Not every Catholic who receives the baptism of the Holy Spirit and joins enthusiastically in prayer meetings with fellow charismatics remains in the movement. One of the veterans of the Paraclete cult, Professor J. Massingberd Ford, remarked that "the Pentecostal experience needn't necessarily be permanent—that you probably enjoy this for two or three years and then pass on to a deeper life within the Church."[3] There is no way of knowing how many people simply "pass through" the cult in this manner and are then replaced by new members.

Besides those who simply lose their initial fervor and stop attending the regular prayer meetings, there are those who leave the Catholic Church, renounce its doctrines and practices, and embrace one of the Protestant pentecostal denominations. One woman from Illinois speaks from experience in this regard: "I am greatly concerned about the many Spirit-filled lay people who are leaving the Church because of a lack of Spirit-filled guidance by priests." A male charismatic from Massachusetts fears that the whole movement may break away from the Church "unless we learn to avoid pride and a sense of separateness from our fellow Catholics." A serious situation has arisen in a California town where "a whole group of 'over-zealous members' separated themselves from the charismatic renewal and because of their anti-Catholic attitudes and behavior have caused many people in our community to disapprove of the renewal."

Touched by God

Comings and goings are manifestations of change in any social movement, but there is also internal spiritual change that involves the membership and the composition of prayer groups. The pentecostal experience is essentially a change of heart, a religious *metanoia*, a conversion experience. The hypothesis that the charismatic renewal has a personal effect on people is an obvious one since the whole movement is geared to changing the lives of participants. Something "happens" to people so that they become committed almost in spite of themselves.[4] "Certainly, in my case," said one of the national leaders, "it is the sort of movement that my training and instincts would have tended to keep me far from. I am involved because I believe that God has touched me and that I have responsibilities as a result of that touch and call."

The growing literature on Catholic pentecostalism is replete with first-person testimony of this touch of God. One priest reports that "I felt as if God took off the top of my head and poured his peace into me and that simultaneously all the junk of my past life was draining out of my feet." A young lady writes that "for me the baptism of the Holy Spirit was a particular moment in my life; a moment when all time seemed to stand still and I truly felt the presence of the reality of Christ." A man tells how he and his wife enrolled in the Spirit seminars in preparation for the night when they were to receive the baptism of the Spirit: "As they prayed over us, and laid hands on us, I felt as if my tongue was swelling up. I wanted to praise God more completely than I had ever before. I wanted to, I wanted to, and I began to praise God aloud with babbling sounds."[5]

Many of these autobiographical anecdotes include protestations of early disbelief and suspicion. Some of them were at first "turned off" by the accounts they heard of strange happenings at prayer meetings. They make it clear that they felt that this kind of thing was not for them; they were often skeptical, even resistant, to invitations from their friends in the movement. Bobbie Cavnar, now a leader of a Texas prayer group, says that at first he thought his son was involved in a Communist plot with his friends in the charismatic renewal and had the group investigated.[6] These preliminary doubts tend to underscore the authenticity of the conversion experience.

While most of these accounts seem to indicate that the touch of God is sudden, unexpected, and even resisted, Gelpi points out that "true conversion is a complex human process, far more complex than the mere experience of God in prayer, the experience of 'Spirit-baptism,' or the reception of any single gift, including the gift of tongues." It should not be confused, he says, with any single religious experience. "The mere fact, for instance, that one seems to experience God with great vividness at a prayer meeting is no assurance that one's heart is truly converted to him."[7]

It is probable that the concept of "peak experience" developed by Abraham Maslow is analogous to the conversion experience of Catholic charismatics. It generally refers to an occurrence that is "particularly striking and significant. It is the type of experience that we cannot easily forget because it was so unusual and different. Peak experiences are those which bring about notable changes of behavior, changes that are profound and lasting. From a peak experience a person might well develop a whole new outlook on life, a different or more meaningful philosophy."[8] This does not deny, however, that religious conversion may also be a gradual process of change over a period of time. O'Connor warns people against the expectation of "instant sanctity," and says that "the majority of spiritual developments, even among Pentecostals, take place quietly and gradually."[9]

It is not the task of the social scientist to attempt to rationalize this mystical *metanoia*, but the data of research indicate that it is preceded by repentance of sins. At the first Pentecost Peter preached to the people in Jerusalem, who asked him what they should do. He told them: "Turn away from your sins, each one of you, and be baptized in the name of Jesus Christ, so that your sins will be forgiven; and you will receive God's gift, the Holy Spirit."[10] All of the respondents to this survey say that they "know how it feels to repent and to experience the forgiveness of sins." All of them say also that they have received the baptism of the Spirit, but not all (86%) report that they have received the gift of speaking in tongues.

Catholic theologians of the charismatic renewal are careful to point out that baptism in the Spirit does not replace sacramental baptism and that speaking in tongues is not a necessary consequence and manifestation of true Spirit baptism. David du Plessis, however, gives a speech to Catholic charismatics in which he says that "God has no grandsons." By this he means that children whose parents had them baptized sacramentally do not become children of God until they have had the conversion experience of Spirit baptism. When this has occurred, its authenticity is guaranteed by the gift of glossolalia, which Catholic theologians call "the least of the gifts."[11]

The conversion experience is, or results in, a kind of special relationship with God. This is indicated by the fact that "a feeling of God's presence in my everyday life" is the principal benefit claimed by the members of the charismatic renewal. Another effect, the certitude that their salvation is assured by their acceptance of Jesus as personal savior, is claimed by more than half (55%) of the respondents. Gelpi warns that "true conversion offers no absolute assurance of salvation. Man remains free before God, before, during, and after the conversion process. Only he who perseveres to the end shall be saved. . . . Any conversion which claims the contrary is suspect."[12]

Most members feel that the mystical experience of conversion places them on a new level of existence. A professional woman from central New York asserts that "my life in the past three years since receiving the baptism of the Holy Spirit has been more rewarding than the previous forty years. My fears and doubts have been replaced by faith, love, peace and joy. The Holy Trinity is no longer a mystery." A well-to-do matron from northern New Jersey writes that "the charismatic renewal has vastly changed my life. I still feel Christ within me and I return His love with a strength not my own. My place in life, as the mother of a family, is all that prevents me from giving up our considerable wealth and following Him."

Quantity and Quality of Change

The questionnaire used in this survey of the pentecostal laity listed nine items of behavior and asked, about each of them: "Since becoming active in the charismatic renewal movement have you done the following things more often,

or less often, than you used to?" Our initial assumption—
that the reported changes were a consequence of membership in the cult—was contested by some respondents who
wrote, "I was always a frequent communicant," or, "I
regularly in the past contributed to the support of my
parish." In other words, there were several items to which
some people wanted to answer neither "more often" nor
"less often," thus implying that there was no need for change.

Another assumption, however, was that membership in
the cult would have a differential influence on people: that
there would be more changes in some forms of behavior
and less in others, and that there would be some persons
who made many changes and others who made few. In
order to make comparisons, we set up three categories based
on the number of changes reported by respondents. Those
who reported seven to nine changes numbered 208 (or 28%).
The largest number were in the middle category—363 (or
49%) who said they had made from four to six changes. The
remainder, 173 persons (or 23%), reported the fewest changes,
from none to three. In crude statistical terms, then, not only
a qualitative change but also a quantitative change occurs
in the lives of these people as a result of their participation
in the renewal movement.

Among the items listed in Table 4.1, there can be no
doubt that reading of the Scriptures is the item of behavior
most emphatically affected by membership in the charismatic renewal. It is probably also one of the main factors
by which pentecostals may be distinguished from conventional Catholics. This is a prayerful, rather than exegetical,
daily practice. Courses in scriptural exegesis are regularly
offered by charismatic leaders in the larger and more organized pentecostal communities. At every prayer meeting we
attended, several members were inspired to read favorite

TABLE 4.1

Percentage of Increase in Selected Activities Brought on by the Charismatic Renewal

Activities performed more often since joining the charismatic renewal	% reporting 7-9 changes (n = 208)	% reporting 4-6 changes (n = 363)	% reporting 0-3 changes (n = 173)
Reading the Scriptures	100	99	96
Receiving Holy Communion	100	93	16
Attending Holy Mass	100	92	16
Visiting the Blessed Sacrament	96	65	17
Personally giving help to poor people	90	63	35
Contributing money to my home parish	90	43	21
Going to Confession	80	26	7
Praying the Rosary	73	17	4
Asking a non-Catholic to join the Church	33	9	3

passages from the Bible. One of the practices taken over from the Protestant pentecostals is that of "cutting the scriptures," that is, opening the Bible at random to see if "God has something to say to you." Cardinal Suenens said he learned about this through his contact with the charismatic renewal, and tried it out in a conversation with Archbishop Ramsey of Canterbury.[13]

At the bottom of Table 4.1, we find that the smallest proportion of the respondents said that since becoming active in the charismatic movement, they had "more often" asked non-Catholics to join the Church. This response also seems to reflect an attitude toward Protestantism that is stronger among charismatics than among conventional Catholics. While one-third of the "most changed" group said they had made efforts to convert people to Catholicism, these efforts seem not to be in accord with the general ecumenical thrust of the members, most of whom want to share prayer life with non-Catholics rather than bring them into the Catholic Church. Some respondents suggested that this question was quite tactless, if not gauche, and that we should have asked whether they were trying to convert Catholics to pentecostalism. A sales manager in Michigan chided us for not noticing that "this movement is making tremendous strides towards a greater love and unity among *all* Christians—the barriers of separation are coming down."[14]

The responses of the people in the third column of Table 4.1—those who made the fewest changes—suggest that the charismatic experience has had practically no effect on their lives. This is not necessarily true, however, because in many cases the quantity of change may not be nearly as important as the quality of change. One of those who reported few changes, a Chicago matron, said, "I can't tell you that becoming a charismatic has made me do these things more often, but I do *strongly* witness that it has greatly enhanced my appreciation of these activities and developed in me even stronger belief in their value." Nevertheless, we hypothesize that willingness or unwillingness to change is accompanied by other characteristics related to the pentecostal movement.

If we pursue this quantitative approach and make further comparisons between the "most changed" group, in column one, and the "least changed," in column three of Table 4.1, we discover several interesting differences between them. The first is that the former appear to have more appreciation for and loyalty to the hierarchy and clergy than the latter.

They are more ready to say (85% to 65%) that the Catholic pentecostal movement cannot go on without the clergy; to acknowledge (84% to 74%) that Pope Paul VI is the infallible Vicar of Christ; and also (64% to 50%) to submit obediently to their bishop were he to prohibit meetings of charismatic prayer groups in the diocese.

The second difference lies in the attitudes of the two groups toward institutional change. The peculiar case seems to be that, in general, those who have made more changes in their personal lives are the most unwilling to approve changes in the Church. Perhaps this demonstrates again that a readiness to accept internal adaptations can be accompanied by a resistance to institutional change. For example, the "most changed" are not as ready as the "least changed" to agree (41% to 61%) that the Church should allow optional marriage for priests. They are not as willing to agree (19% to 36%) that the Church should support the Women's Liberation Movement; nor are they as prepared (21% to 32%) to approve the use of the pill by married women.

The third difference centers on beliefs and behavior that may be called characteristically pentecostal. Certain definitive elements of membership in the movement, such as a feeling of repentance for sins and baptism in the Spirit, are shared by changers and non-changers, as well as by all participants in the cult. Those who have experienced the greatest change, however, are also more likely (91% to 75%) to report that they have received the gift of speaking in tongues. They are also more ready (81% to 64%) to express the belief that the Second Coming of the Lord is imminent.

Newcomers versus Old-timers

The above attempt to account for differential quantitative change among members of the pentecostal movement is not fully satisfactory. We have made the obvious comment that the charismatic experience is, by its very nature, a "reform" of the individual's spiritual life. Our hypothesis, that the "more charismatic" persons in the movement would also report the greatest number of changes, is only partly supported by the evidence. We can approach the question in another way, however, by trying to discover whether or not there is a correlation between the length of time people have been in the movement and the number of changes they report.

TABLE 4.2

Proportions of Newcomers, Intermediates, and Old-timers Reporting Various Degrees of Change

	% New-comers (n = 232)	% Inter-mediates (n = 410)	% Old-timers (n = 102)
Most change (7 to 9)	22	30	34
Medium change (4 to 6)	46	50	49
Least change (0 to 3)	32	20	17

The statistical comparisons in Table 4.2 tend to support the notion that those who have been longest in the movement will have experienced the most numerous changes. We find that twice as many of the old-timers are in the category of most change (34%) as are in the category of least change (17%). The newcomers, however, are more likely to report least change (32%) than most change (22%). In other words, about one-third of the old-timers are among those who made the greatest number of changes, while about one-third of the newcomers are among those who made the least.

Two contrasting hypothetical explanations may be offered as "reasons" for some members reporting greater frequency of change. The first is that the newcomers, those who have joined the movement within the last year, may be so enthusiastic and excited about the charismatic experience that they will immediately want to make as many changes as possible. The opposite hypothesis suggests that the old-timers, those who have been with the movement for more than three years, will have learned from their associates that changes should be numerous and thorough. The tentative conclusions we draw from the data in Table 4.2 reinforce the latter supposition, but we must test further the expectation that the longer a person is in the movement, the greater will be its effect on him.

Becoming Better Catholics

Bernardine Abbott writes that "in essence, the Catholic Pentecostal becomes a 'better' Catholic" and says also that "pentecostal spirituality tends to lead an individual toward even closer ties with his historic church than he had previously maintained."[15] Two pieces of evidence are provided to substantiate the validity of this statement. The first is that Catholic pentecostals "live more fully the sacramental life of the Church." The second is that they "become more obedient to the Church," that is, the hierarchy. The research data should then demonstrate that the longer a person is in the movement, the better Catholic he should become.

How does one determine whether Catholic lay people become better Catholics, or become different kinds of Catholics, through participation in the charismatic cult? We have seen that ecumenical mingling with Protestant pentecostals has resulted in widespread acceptance of certain heterodox beliefs which are rejected by orthodox Catholics. The paraliturgical practices taken over from Protestant pentecostals are judged by many to be peculiarly "new"; certainly they are different from those by which Catholics express their devotion at Sunday Mass in the conventional parish church. We have been assured by theological experts that these forms of religious worship are acceptably orthodox, although they have not been in common practice among either the laity or the clergy.[16] Whether they make people better Catholics, or whether only better Catholics practice them, is a question beyond the scope of our study.

We deliberately went further than this in our survey and asked about some of the "traditional" Catholic religious devotions. We were curious to know whether the new forms were replacing the old or simply supplementing them. We found that the veterans of the movement are "better" in this regard than the novices. A larger proportion of them (old-timers 65%, newcomers 55%) say that they visit the Blessed Sacrament more frequently than they used to. They also receive Holy Communion more often (80% to 71%) and attend Mass more regularly (80% to 67%) since joining in the charismatic renewal. This is convincing proof that there is a deepening of the sacramental life.

There is one religious practice, however, that elicits a negative response in a minority of both categories. More of the old-timers (23%) than of the newcomers (13%) report that they go to confession *less* often than they did before becoming involved in prayer meetings. One woman, an old-timer from Indiana, says: "Since my baptism in the Holy Spirit, I go to confession less often, but definitely more effectively. For the first time I realize the grace imparted here. I await the occasion of a Spirit-filled priest and have a greater love for this sacrament now, because of the Holy Spirit in my life." Another old-timer, also a lady from the Midwest, remarks: "I feel that my sins are forgiven in the prayers at the beginning of Mass. But when I go to the confessional I often come away very troubled because the priest misinterprets what I am confessing. However, I always know when a Spirit-filled priest is there."

We can only guess at the extent to which the charismatic experience, by focusing on an intimate and trusting relationship with God, might tend to de-emphasize the need for sacramental confession among pentecostal Catholics, yet there does appear to be some influence in this direction. More of the newcomers (53%) than of the old-timers (38%) report that they go to confession as frequently now as they did before joining the charismatic prayer groups. Parish priests commonly state that while the number of confessions has decreased, there has been a steady increase in the number of parishioners who receive Holy Communion.

One of the most notable of the changes made by Catholic pentecostals is the replacement of many previous devotional practices. It is almost as though a cultic void occurred when, after the Second Vatican Council, Catholics stopped attending novenas, forty-hours devotions, the Way of the Cross, Benediction of the Blessed Sacrament, holy hours, and First Friday devotions. The faithful seemed to lose interest in these non-eucharistic religious services, which had once been very popular. The devotional need was apparently not satisfied by the many changes in the celebration of the Mass. The people wanted more, and many of them found it by taking over the devotional and paraliturgical practices of Protestant pentecostalism.

One may ask also what happened to the traditional devotions to the Blessed Virgin among these people, whose main preoccupation seems to be with the Paraclete.[17] One group in Louisiana reports that it concludes its afternoon prayer meetings with the recitation of the Rosary. Only three out of ten report that they say the Rosary more often than they used to; while nine out of ten had never participated in the Block Rosary. Table 4.1 shows that the rosary devotion is far down the list of favorite religious practices—indeed, more of the old-timers (15%) than of the newcomers (7%) say that they pray it less often than they did before joining the charismatic renewal.

In other words, Marian devotion is not a feature of the Catholic pentecostal movement, a point which was made at the 1973 International Conference by Father Howard Rafferty in his seminar on "Mary in the Charismatic Renewal." Cardinal Suenens, at the end of the homily he preached at the concluding liturgy of the Conference, said that he had a "little secret" to confide in the people. It was that "unity with the Spirit is in our unity with Mary, the mother of God. Christ was born out of the Spirit by the cooperation of Mary. On the day of Pentecost, the Church was born the same way: Mary was there helping the apostles to receive the Spirit of God."[18] It was almost as though he were hesitantly suggesting that Mary should be restored to the prayer life of charismatics.

Changing Class Composition

Catholic pentecostalism has been called a "middle-class movement," and this feature sets it apart from the earlier Protestant pentecostal sects, whose membership derived from the lower economic classes.[19] The social-background statistics of the present survey tend to confirm this generalization. Only three out of ten (29%) respondents classify themselves as blue-collar workers, while four out of ten (39%) claim professional or managerial occupations. There appears to have been a downward shift in class status as the movement has developed—the difference being that the old-timers (47%) are more likely than the newcomers (36%) to be in the upper occupational strata. Among the newer members we find a higher proportion (35%) of blue-collar workers than among the veterans (20%). It seems that the movement is now attracting more people from the working class.

A young steelworker from Missouri who has been going to prayer meetings for less than a year complained that the questions we asked were directed mainly at "university people." He suggested that we ask such questions as: "Do you belong to a labor union? Are you trying to improve working conditions on the job? Are you active in helping the ghetto poor?" It is unfortunate that our questions should seem to be class-oriented, or of concern only to better-educated people. It is also possible that our contact persons selected mainly the better-educated members to answer the questionnaires. We are certainly aware that we have not reached a random sample of the membership, and we suspect that the large proportion of blue-collar workers are not represented in this study. Indeed, one sixty-year-old male remarked, "I dare say that you will wind up with a very high percentage of leaders in your sampling procedure."

Since university people at Duquesne, Ann Arbor, and Notre Dame were so deeply involved in the modern beginnings of Catholic pentecostalism, it is to be expected that those who have been longest in the renewal would be rather highly educated and have concomitantly higher occupational status.[20] The percentage difference among those who attended college (old-timers 75%, newcomers 65%) may not be statistically significant, but the difference in social-class background is indicated also by the fact that the veterans are more likely (28% to 16%) to have fathers who went to college. If there is a trend in this regard, it appears to be in the direction of involving more members from working-class families.

Perhaps a more significant trend is suggested by the nature of the members' experience in higher education, that is, Catholic or non-Catholic. The newer members who have been to college tend to come from non-Catholic campuses: half of the old-timers who were college people, as compared to 38% of the newcomers, attended Catholic institutions of higher learning. We can only speculate on the reason for this difference. It is possible that the chaplains on the Catholic campuses can satisfy the religious needs of their students with the more traditional religious services, while students on the non-Catholic campus may be more open to the paraliturgical practices of the pentecostal movement.

At any rate, the spiritual attraction of the charismatic renewal, like that of the Catholic Church, is proclaimed to be inclusive and universal, reaching out to all social classes. The earlier Protestant pentecostal sects were unquestionably attractive to the working masses and in some instances became what Niebuhr called the "churches of the disinherited."[21] A classic example is the manner in which the movement spread among the working poor of Chile earlier in this century, much to the puzzlement of the Catholic clergy.[22] Perhaps it is to the puzzlement of social scientists that the contemporary American pentecostal renewal took hold first in the Catholic middle class.

Shifting Sources of Recruitment

While the great majority (86%) of the charismatic lay people were "born" Catholics and more than half (60%) had attended parochial elementary school, they probably had had little experience with intense prayer life and practices

74

before joining the renewal movement. Except for the small handful (11%) who had "tried out" and left a seminary, convent, or novitiate, these people had probably followed the traditional religious practices common to the American Catholic laity. Further, while the movement has definitely been influenced by Protestant pentecostalism, there is no indication that the converts to Catholicism among our respondents (14%) brought any of this influence with them from their former denominations.

Without attempting to retell the story of how the contemporary Catholic charismatic renewal began, O'Connor remarks that "a wave of enthusiasm for bible vigils and prayer meetings had gone across the country during the early 1960's."[23] Also, well before the opening of the Second Vatican Council in 1962 there was widespread interest and participation in the cursillo movement. The literature on Catholic pentecostalism mentions prominently the early strategic significance of the cursillo movement—indeed, suggests strongly that in some sense the charismatic renewal is an outgrowth of the cursillo. Some of the most vocal pentecostal spokesmen and lay leaders of renewal were active in the cursillo before becoming involved in initiating Catholic pentecostalism.[24]

In this survey, then, we expected to find that large numbers of our respondents would have been recruited from the cursillo movement, but this is not the case—only one-fourth had followed this route. Nevertheless, more of the old-timers (37%) than of the newcomers (19%) had previously participated in this spiritual group experience. The charismatic renewal is still recruiting members from cursillo (15% of the newcomers are still in it; 4% used to be). Among the old-time members, however, cursillo no longer seems to have the attraction it once had (10% of them are still in it, but

75

27% have left it). This is an example of religious change, or of "passing through" one religious movement into another.

Our research findings indicate that the Christian Family Movement is an equally fertile source of recruitment for the charismatic renewal. Here again, a larger proportion of the old-timers (38%) than of the newcomers (22%) had been participants in the Christian Family Movement. The shifting out of CFM, however, has been greater than in the case of cursillo. Only 3% of the veterans and 5% of the novices report that they are still active members of CFM. While we have no comparable statistics on the memberships of cursillo and CFM, it is probably safe to say that these two Catholic movements are on the decline while Catholic pentecostalism continues to flourish.

Women are apparently easier to recruit than men. The charismatic renewal, like all Catholic organizations and movements that are open to women, attracts more female than male adherents. Although most of the organizing early "founders" of Catholic pentecostalism in the United States were male, there have always and everywhere been more women than men among the membership. Our survey sample does not reflect the sex ratio of the membership because we attempted to obtain as many male as female respondents. There is a suggestion in the data, however, that women remain more faithful than men over the years. Among the old-timers answering the questionnaire, 57% are female. This proportion was reversed among the newcomers, of whom 56% are male. While the women seem likely to stay in the charismatic movement longer than the men, it also seems likely that a deliberate effort is being made at the present time to recruit a larger membership of males.

Going Conservative

Has membership in the charismatic renewal had any effect on the social thinking of the participants? Has it changed them in this regard? Theoretically, the traditional differences between progressives and reactionaries should disappear under the unifying grace of the Holy Spirit. In the actual prayer meetings of Catholic pentecostals, there appears to be no controversy or conflict over social issues— probably because such issues are not raised. The business at hand is the praise and glory of God. Nevertheless, in response to our questionnaire, the great majority of lay Catholic charismatics express approval of "liberal" programs like medicare, open housing, and higher minimum wages, and there is practically no difference here between the attitudes of old-timers and newcomers.

The majority of both categories also show favorable attitudes in the matter of American race relations. Three-quarters of both old-timers and newcomers approve of the civil-rights movement, and an even higher proportion of both (86%) say that they favor racially integrated schools. There is a marked difference in response, however, when we ask about their personal involvement in interracial movements, with the old-timers twice as likely (32%) as the newcomers (16%) to report that they are now, or have been, participants. While these percentages are small—suggesting that the great majority of Catholic pentecostals are not social activists—they indicate that the charismatic renewal is now attracting even fewer activists in race relations. The old-timers are also more likely (25%) than the newcomers (15%) to say that they give active support to Cesar Chavez's grape and lettuce boycotts.

There is a curious reversal of attitudes, however, when

we ask certain questions about the clergy and the Church. On these matters there is a small percentage difference that consistently shows the old-timers to be more conservative than the newcomers. In response to the statement that "priests have a place on picket lines," more of the newcomers (63%) than the old-timers (57%) are in agreement. Again, more of the newcomers (60%) than of the veterans (50%) think that "the Church should lead in social protest movements." Only a minority (29%) of all respondents holds that the Church should support women's liberation, but more of the newcomers (33%) than of the old-timers (28%) hold this position. A professional woman from California states the "conservative" position as well as anyone: "I strongly disagree with direct involvement of the Church with some of the social and political issues. I think this should be an individual decision always."

It has been suggested that the "better" Catholics are those who are most loyal to the clergy and the hierarchy. There is no intention here of suggesting that the more conservative—or the more liberal—a person is, the "more Catholic" he becomes. We find that about three-fourths of both old-timers and newcomers agree that the charismatic renewal cannot go on without the clergy. There is a significant difference, however, on the delicate question of the charismatics' relations with the bishops of their dioceses. The newcomers appear to be more independent and brash in this area: they are twice as likely (60%) as the old-timers (30%) to say that they would continue to hold their prayer meetings even if the bishop issued a prohibition against them.

One can only speculate on whether the "newer" membership, with its greater independence from the hierarchy and its willingness to encourage the Church's leadership in social protest, will influence the general attitudes of the charismatic renewal, or whether these newcomers will themselves eventually conform to the attitudes of the experienced old-timers. It is too soon to say whether the "routinization of charisma"—to use Max Weber's phrase—has begun to set in among the veterans of the movement. There is no reason to doubt, however, that the "charismatic movement" is becoming embodied "in institutional structures to render it continuously present and available."[25]

5

Personal Comfort and
Social Challenge

Every committed Christian—and perhaps every religious believer—is bothered by the tension between the sacred and the profane, the spiritual and the material.[1] The saints themselves, and those who compose their biographies, discourse at great length on the perennial need to find a personal balance between action and contemplation, between work and prayer. The tension is not always relaxed, nor the balance achieved, through the popular nostrum: "Pray as though everything depends on God, and work as though everything depends on oneself."

This dualistic tension is in evidence too when we look with concern at the major social problems of contemporary life. "Whereas one man looking out on the chaos of the world calls for reform, the other calls for contemplation: one says, Who could tolerate such injustice? The other says, Who would not rejoice that there is another world? One says, Give these people the conditions of a decent life; the other says, Teach them to read the Bible."[2] This is not a contrast between an ignorant, hard-hearted man and a knowledgeable, magnanimous man. It is the difference between two perspectives on the same disorderly and disturbed world.

The Pentecostal Dilemma

American Catholic pentecostals are probably as aware as other people are of the suffering and injustice that abound in society. They are not like the occupants of Pierre Berton's *Comfortable Pew*, who are more or less satisfied with the status quo,[3] but who "need comfort and consolation when the cares of secular society become oppressive."[4] The pentecostals are not satisfied with the world as it is, but they have no intention of trying to change it through organized collective action. Their basic conviction is that reform starts at home, in one's heart, and somehow spills over into other homes and other hearts until all of society is reformed.

The implication in this dilemma is that the thoroughly religious person must somehow be conservative in his social thinking while the dedicated social activist must somehow dilute his religious commitment. There is indeed evidence that some people substitute social action for prayer and that some prayerful people shun social action. Jeffrey Hadden thinks there is a "gathering storm" in the Protestant churches brought on by the ministers whose serious doubts about theological doctrines lead them to try to engage their parishioners in social action programs.[5] These ministers often discover that the laity wants the comfort and security of religious belief rather than the challenge and insecurity of social action. Another study—by Glock, Ringer, and Babbie —finds a similar dilemma in the contemporary Episcopal Church: parishioners with the deepest religious commitment are seldom persuaded by the Church to make an equally deep commitment to the solution of social problems.[6] The dual role of organized religion—to save souls and to save society—splits into separate roles that are sometimes in conflict.

We may well ask whether the burgeoning Catholic charismatic renewal is faced with this same dilemma. Do the members focus so much on God that their eyes are turned away from the world around them? Catholic pentecostals are pious, prayerful people who enjoy an intimate relationship with God and a profound awareness of His presence in their lives. They receive comfort in their contemplation. They appear to confirm the generalization that a contemplative makes an improbable activist, and that the more contact one has with people the less contact one is likely to have with God.

Some leaders of the charismatic renewal, Harold Cohen and Donald Gelpi among them, do not subscribe to this peculiar thesis. They insist that you cannot separate love of God from love of fellow man, that social concern is a manifestation of divine concern. In his keynote address to the 1973 International Conference of Charismatics at Notre Dame University, Father Cohen made it clear that Catholic pentecostals have to be concerned about all social problems: war and peace, prison conditions, urban ghettos and slum housing, racial injustice, migrant workers, and every other human need and problem.[7]

Yet, in a seminar at the same conference, Susan B. Anthony complained that when you suggest social action to charismatics you are greeted with "silence and withdrawal." She reported that her prayer group, in Boca Raton, Florida, holds an additional weekly meeting for members who are concerned about social problems.[8] National leaders of the movement are sensitive to the charge that Catholic pente-

82

costal groups do not turn their attention to the social evils of the times. Bishop Joseph McKinney says that he is deeply impressed with the spiritual renewal generated by Catholic pentecostalism, but that he continues to "look for signs that it inflames its members to engage in genuine social action."[9] Francis MacNutt writes that "we must admit that there is justice to the claim that pentecostal people as a group have not distinguished themselves in the overall quest for social justice." He is convinced that "a transformation of the structures of society is needed," but he confesses that "this issue is not touched in charismatic circles."[10]

Despite these recommendations from the leadership, the primary thrust of the movement continues to be the personal sanctification of its members. In answering a question about social involvement, one thirty-eight-year-old male said: "One must develop a personal relationship with the Lord through prayer first or he will be of no value to himself, the Church or all of mankind in general." The Church too should be primarily interested in the salvation of souls: a thirty-five-year-old chemist states that "although the Church should be concerned with social injustice, its primary function is not social action but spreading the good news of salvation in Jesus Christ and His presence today, tomorrow and always."

If there is a charismatic "mentality" in this regard among Catholic pentecostals, it includes a desire to "put first things first." The prime purpose in this life is to praise, love, and serve God so that we can be happy with Him in the afterlife. This is nothing new among believers of all religions. Within two centuries of the resurrection of Christ, thousands of His followers had become contemplatives in the deserts of Egypt. There have always been people who put God first by fleeing the world. No one is suggesting that American charismatics want to go that far, or that they want to form a new religious order or to establish a separate, otherworldly, religious sect. They are orthodox, devout, lay Catholics who seek spiritual regeneration in their daily lives.

Liberal and Conservative

It is sometimes said that the experience of Spirit-baptism renders the terms "liberal" and "conservative" increasingly meaningless.[11] Several of the founding fathers of the movement who had been activists in socially progressive movements and crusades appear to have lost interest in them since receiving the charismatic gifts. From the point of view of social action, they can be said to have switched from the liberal to the conservative position. Nouwen likens this to the philosophy of the Yogi, who insists above all on inner purification. "It is not surprising, therefore, to find that the Pentecostal, like the Yogi, has often been accused of being aloof and indifferent to the great social problems of war, poverty, pollution, segregation, social injustice, and crime, and of having escaped into a personal garden where he can concentrate on his own soul, experience the stirrings of the Spirit, and make his own conversion the criterion for the solutions of the problems of this world."[12]

This Christian Yogi philosophy may persuade Catholic pentecostals to withdraw from social action, but it does not necessarily neutralize their social attitudes. Indeed, we found that most of them do express progressive social attitudes, especially in the matter of racial justice. The great majority are in favor of the black civil rights movement, of racially integrated schooling, and of the enactment of legislation for racially open housing. Most of them think that the Medicare program is a good idea and also approve an extension of the minimum-wage legislation. Where they are not socially progressive, as in their attitudes toward the ordination of women and the equal rights amendment, they are probably taking their cue from the American bishops, who still take a dim view of women's liberation.[13]

With the research data at hand we are able to establish categories that separate the liberal respondents from the conservative. It ought to be clear that we are not here dealing with the distinction between radical (liberal) theology and reactionary (conservative) theology among the Catholic pentecostals. This kind of question can safely be left to the theologians of the movement and to their theological critics. We are looking at these polar terms—liberal and conservative—from a sociological perspective, that is, with the intention of establishing the presence or absence of socially "progressive" ideas and attitudes among the lay membership. We built into the questionnaire several crucial items concerning the Catholic Church's stance on social activism, and these serve as criteria for constructing liberal-conservative categories.

According to this rough form of measurement, we define a liberal charismatic as a person who agrees with all three of the following statements: (a) priests have a place on picket lines; (b) the Church should lead in social protest movements; (c) the Church should support women's liberation. The conservative charismatic is the person who disagrees with all three. Among the 744 respondents to our survey we found 155 (21%) who accept all three statements, and 219 (29%) who reject all three. This means, of course, that half (370) of our respondents can be termed "moderates" —those who accept two of the statements (pro-liberals) and those who accept only one (pro-conservatives), but who do not fit our polar definitions.

The question about the Church's support of women's

liberation is, in a sense, the "key" to the distinction between liberal and conservative pentecostals. More than half (57%) of all respondents agree that priests ought to take their place on picket lines; a majority (54%) also agree that the Church should take the lead in social protest movements. If we had employed only these two criteria, the liberals would have outnumbered the conservatives. The "progressive" notion, however, that the Church should support women's liberation got a favorable reply from only a minority (29%) of all respondents. This was the stumbling block for many charismatics whose attitudes on other social issues were fairly liberal.

The statistics in Table 5.1 provide ample evidence of the differential in social attitudes and of the consistency of these attitudes in both polar categories. For each of the six social issues listed there we see a significantly more progressive response from the liberals than from the conservatives. One is forced then to question the notion that the experi-

TABLE 5.1

Percentage of Approval Expressed by Liberals, Moderates, and Conservatives on Selected Social Issues

	% Liberal (n = 155)	% Moderate (n = 370)	% Conservative (n = 219)
Civil rights movement	96	81	56
Laws for open housing	88	78	56
Optional marriage for priests	70	51	43
Higher social welfare payments	54	30	16
Popular election of bishops	47	34	27
Use of pill by married women	39	27	21

ence of baptism in the Spirit and of the other charismatic gifts renders this dichotomy "meaningless." The comparative data prove conclusively that social attitudes may be retained even after the pentecostal experience and that attachment to the charismatic renewal need not neutralize strongly held social attitudes.

Attitudes and Heterodox Beliefs

There can be no doubt that both liberals and conservatives are authentic pentecostals; both report that they have experienced repentance and forgiveness of sins, received the baptism of the Spirit and the gift of speaking in tongues, and now regularly read the Holy Scriptures. The general sharing in these basic characteristics of genuine membership, however, does not preclude differences in other charismatic characteristics. There are certain notions prevalent among Catholic pentecostals that are generally not held by conventional Catholics. In another place we have called these "heterodox" beliefs, and we can see in the movement itself no inherent reason for a difference of opinion between liberals and conservatives concerning these beliefs.[14] Nevertheless, they differ significantly.

The comparative statistics in Table 5.2 demonstrate that those who are socially liberal are much less likely than the socially conservative to accept these heterodox beliefs. There is a spread of thirty percentage points on the statement that the Second Coming of Christ is imminent, and a spread of twenty percentage points on the notion that the Spirit speaks to the heart rather than to the mind. It is true that these concepts have been brought over from Protestant pentecostalism and tend to infect all Catholic charismatics, but it is clear that the liberals have been better able than the conservatives to resist them.

TABLE 5.2

Percentage of Acceptance by Liberals, Moderates, and Conservatives of Three Pentecostal Beliefs

	% Liberal (n = 155)	% Moderate (n = 370)	% Conservative (n = 219)
The Second Coming of Christ is imminent	53	72	83
Accepting Jesus means I am already saved	50	55	58
Spirit speaks to the heart, not the mind	41	48	61

Let us turn from these innovative pentecostal notions and look at the religious practices that have been fairly traditional among Catholics. Here we are testing the hypothesis that socially conservative people are more likely than liberals to be faithful to religious practices. The statistics in Table 5.3 demonstrate a consistent difference in this regard and tend to prove the hypothesis.

Since it is obviously true that the lay membership of the renewal movement is composed of both liberals and conservatives—and those in between—we had best look outside of pentecostalism for the genesis of these differences in social attitudes. It is a commonplace of sociological analysis that differences in age, sex, and education help to account for differences in social attitudes. In the present comparison we find that more of the liberals (34%) than of the conservatives (24%) are under thirty-five years of age. More of the liberals (54%) than of the conservatives (47%) are males. Twice as many of the liberals (55%) as of the conservatives

TABLE 5.3

Proportions of Liberals, Moderates, and Conservatives Reporting Increase in Five Activities

	% Liberal (n = 155)	% Moderate (n = 370)	% Con- servative (n = 219)
Receiving Holy Communion	72	78	79
Attending Holy Mass	72	77	78
Visiting the Blessed Sacrament	56	64	65
Going to Confession	30	39	37
Praying the Rosary	23	31	32

(27%) are college graduates.[15] It may be worth noting also that fewer of the liberals (7%) than of the conservatives (15%) are converts to the Catholic Church.

Up to this point in our analysis of lay Catholic charismatics we have found that the majority exhibit fairly favorable social attitudes, especially on the major issues of the day. We have seen also, however, that there are sharp differences between the liberals and the conservatives and that these differences correlate with both pentecostal beliefs and traditional Catholic practices. Finally, then, the differences in social attitudes must be attributed mainly to the non-pentecostal factors of age, sex, and education.

Social Activism

The general expectation is that social attitudes will be seen to be related in some way to participation by liberals in social action and to non-participation by conservatives. Even though membership in the charismatic renewal is generally compatible with favorable social attitudes, we find that fewer than one out of five of all respondents have been or are now involved in voter registration campaigns, peace demonstrations, grape or lettuce boycotts, the interracial movement, or the National Conference of Christians and Jews. The comparisons in Table 5.4, however, demonstrate that the large differences in social attitudes shown by the two groups are accompanied by large proportional differences in their participation in such movements.

TABLE 5.4

Proportions of Liberals, Moderates, and Conservatives Who Have Been, or Are Now, Involved in Social Action Movements

	% Liberal (n = 155)	% Moderate (n = 370)	% Conservative (n = 219)
Interracial movement	37	21	5
Grape or lettuce boycott	32	16	4
Anti-war demonstration	21	9	1
Voter registration campaign	19	11	7
Conference of Christians and Jews	8	6	4
An "underground" Church	6	4	1

The comparative data here tell us more than the obvious fact that people with conservative social attitudes are not likely to engage in organized social action, while those with liberal social attitudes are at least more likely than the conservatives to do so. When I presented these findings to a Catholic pentecostal audience, I was challenged by the claim that Catholic charismatics are neither more nor less involved in social action programs than are conventional Catholics.[16] We have no comparable data from a control group of non-charismatic Catholics, but we may speculate that this low record of participation is probably typical of the American Catholic laity. Whether or not this is true, however, it would probably not be inappropriate to endorse Bishop McKinney's suggestion that charismatics ought to be more active in social reform movements.

Why is it, then, that the liberal charismatics seem to have a higher quotient of social concern than the average Catholic laity? Before analyzing the potential modes of social action, let us look at two contrasting points of view offered by Catholic lay pentecostals, both giving reasons for avoiding social activism. A thirty-five-year-old housewife from Illinois wrote: "I used to be a social rebel and believed that protest movements were necessary because the establishment, the society and the Church needed drastic changes. Now I believe the answer is in knowing Jesus Christ and following the lead of the Spirit. It gives me a *peace* I never had in the face of all this injustice and taught me dependence on *God*. Taking matters into our hands never solved any social problem." This woman has clearly been influenced by pentecostalism to abandon organized social protest and reform.

A contrasting explanation comes from a young, unmarried secretary from Minnesota who does not want to be charged with "social irresponsibility" for answering the questionnaire in the way she did. "There is a strong movement among radicals in my age group to get out of organized and political social action and to get into an investigation of alternative life styles and a reevaluation of consciousness-raising. For me personally, this shift coincided with my decision to move into charismatic community." For this twenty-three-year-old "radical," pentecostalism seems to be a haven from the disillusionment brought on by frustrated efforts at social reform.

These two women are in our liberal category; they profess progressive social attitudes, but both are among those who "used to be" active in several protest and reform movements. They are still deeply interested in the renewal of the Church itself and of the larger civil society. They have accepted the pentecostal principle that "the person who strives for justice must himself be totally transformed in Christ."[17] There could be no quarrel with this long-range program of personal preparation for the eventual transformation of social structures *if* such a transformation could be shown to be its purpose. The general implication of the pentecostal philosophy, however, is that the external structures and systems of both Church and society really do not matter, that somehow "God will take care of them." Meanwhile, the charismatic renewal movement tends to withdraw its members from the struggle for social justice and to blunt their zeal for social reform.

Levels of Social Action

Through personal contact with many charismatic lay people and conversations with clerical leaders of the renewal, we have been able to produce a rough typology of social action at three levels. The first poses the question of whether the local prayer group should organize itself to work for the alleviation of one or more social problems. A charismatic sister from Connecticut, a nurse who is personally involved in reforming the health services in her city, is convinced that this approach would be the death of her prayer community. She insists that reconciliation, peace, harmony, and unity are essential to the continuing vitality of the charismatic group.

Phil O'Mara, who is both a social activist and a prayerful charismatic, has seen disruption, bitterness, quarreling, and even animosity develop in Catholic religious movements when attempts have been made to formulate programs of social action. He does not want this to happen in the charismatic renewal. "It will take a good deal of thought, prayer, and study to do something practical in the social order while avoiding conflicts that would rip the movement apart in a particular place or on the national level."[18] He points a warning finger at the controversial experiences of the Liturgical Conference, the Young Christian Students, the Young Christian Workers, the Christian Family Movement, and the Cursillo Movement. He feels that the charismatic renewal is too young and fragile to engage in social controversy.

The need for internal harmony, for peaceful Catholic unity, is considered to be fundamental to the local prayer community. The members are not likely to fight about theological and scriptural interpretations, but they are convinced that concrete proposals for organized social action would tear them apart.[19] The findings of our survey demonstrate that despite their spiritual unity, the members have not abandoned their diverse political and social convictions. In their religious convictions they are basically of one-mind-in-the-Spirit, but in social matters they still range along the whole continuum from very liberal to very conservative. It would be a rare and probably very small prayer group that could get its members to agree on a specific, organized, social action program.

Edward O'Connor frankly describes this dilemma as it developed in the rapidly growing Notre Dame prayer community. Some individuals and subgroups engaged in apostolic activities to which most members were not attracted, and the result was internal friction that was sometimes "painful." He reports that "there is no apostolate or work

93

proper to the whole community except the weekly prayer meeting. This has disturbed some, who feel that the community as such ought to have a ministry. 'God does not form a Christian community just to hold prayer meetings,' they sometimes declare. But although several people feel that the present state of things is an incomplete, unfulfilled beginning, no one has been able to propose a work to which the whole community could feasibly dedicate itself."[20]

An exception to this generalization is related by Father Rick Thomas, who is a charismatic leader of prayer groups in El Paso and Juarez. He tells of the Christmas dinner in 1972 that he and his members brought across the border to share with poor people living in the garbage dump of Juarez. Two weeks later thirty members of the local prayer groups made a covenant agreement to live in community. Now they make a weekly visit, on Saturday, to bring assistance to these dump dwellers. "Food and clothing and housing deal with some of the need: prayer is beginning to deal with others. There have been a number of striking physical healings. We have also prayed in faith for a well somewhere near by, so that these people may have water. God is going to do something great."[21]

The second level of social action, as indicated in Table 5.4, is that on which a minority of lay Catholic pentecostals actually operate. Whether these few members are inspired by the social Gospel or by charismatic religious motivation, they involve themselves in a variety of social action programs and protest movements. They participate in "outside" groups, that is, groups outside and away from the people in the renewal community. They cooperate with other citizens, non-Catholics and non-charismatics, to alleviate the injustices of the larger society.

This is a "safe" way for the individual pentecostal to

engage in social action without causing the friction of which O'Connor speaks or endangering the survival of the prayer community. By and large, however, the great majority of lay charismatics do not participate in reform and protest movements. Among other reasons for their abstention, there appears to be the feeling that secular society is corrupt, that social structures are incorrigible, and that the only solution is the formation of separate Christian communities. "When society as a whole cannot be expected to accept Christianity, then it is necessary to form communities within society to make Christian life possible."[22] This "escape" mentality is expressed by one of the chief pentecostal spokesmen, Stephen Clark, in his book, *Building Christian Communities*.

The evolution of local prayer groups into tightly knit and exclusive charismatic communities was described with marked enthusiasm by Bertil Ghezzi. The so-called covenant community at Ann Arbor, with its subcommunities and households, or "living groups," is the best developed and most highly organized, and it was thought by some to be the model for similar developments in other parts of the country. Ghezzi later had second thoughts about this: "Not every prayer group is or even ought to become a Christian community. Becoming a community involves putting people's lives together in a more total and daily way than most prayer groups have the resources to do effectively."[23]

Other leaders of the renewal, however, have been concerned over the lack of individual involvement in organized social reform movements. James Burke says that he has "heard repeatedly one criticism of the charismatic renewal: that its members are not involved in the work of liberation, but have an individualistic spirituality which is an escape from the real world and its enormous problems."[24] Francis

MacNutt comments further that "the charismatic renewal has not spoken to the 'liberal' Christians of all denominations who see Christ in the poor and who are determined to restructure society to help the oppressed. In fact, there seems to be a strong mutual suspicion between charismatic Christians and those Christians who are social activists."[25]

Corporal Works of Mercy

If the local prayer group chooses not to organize itself for concrete social action for fear of disruption, and if the great majority of individual charismatics are reluctant to participate in other reform movements, there remains the third level of social action, that of personal concern and care for the needs of others. One may say that there is a "spillover" of Christian love in that most of the members report an increase in their performance of the corporal works of mercy since they joined the charismatic renewal. Some prayer groups call this the "ministry of love," and it apparently takes as many forms as there are human needs to be met: working with alcoholics and drug addicts, preparing meals for shut-ins, visiting the sick and lonely in hospitals and nursing homes, sitting with the elderly, and providing food, clothing, and money to needy families.

This personal concern for the needs of others contrasts with the charitable activities of members of the conventional Catholic parish, in which the sense of neighborliness tends to be dissipated. The parish provides formal channels for charity like the Saint Vincent de Paul Society and the "drives" for money and food to be put into baskets for the poor at Thanksgiving and Christmas. Most parishioners thus experience charity as an impersonal activity largely effectuated by their designated surrogates or representatives. The members of the charismatic prayer group are inspired to respond personally, rather than through a group representative, to the poor and needy. Their ingroup solidarity allows them to reach many more people than they could have in a conventional parish. The majority of members seem to be middle-class Catholics with no besetting financial problems of their own, but they alert each other to the needy cases that come to their attention.

In several of the larger charismatic prayer communities, there is a person, or a small subcommittee, whose special ministry it is to find "needy cases" in the same city. These "cases" are then distributed, as it were, to married couples among the membership, and each couple assumes the responsibility of providing care for those less fortunate than themselves. In many instances the need is that of a family in distress; in other cases it may be that of some neglected individual to whom direct material and spiritual aid is to be given. This personal involvement in the performance of corporal works of mercy seems to be a new experience for most of the middle-class Catholic pentecostals.

The pentecostal approach to one social problem, that of youthful delinquency, is outlined in Wilkerson's *The Cross and the Switchblade* and in Pulkingham's description of his work with young people at Holy Redeemer in Houston.[26] In neither of these instances was there an organized professional approach to the problem of delinquency. The youth on drugs, or in the corner gang, or in trouble with the police, is seen as an individual in need of personal care, prayer, and rehabilitation, and special solicitude is given to pregnant teen-aged girls. Here again, for the most part, the members are not dealing with their own sons and daughters, but with strangers, yet they are willing to spend not only money but personal time and effort in an attempt to alleviate the misery of such young unfortunates.

97

It is at this point that the "healing" ministry of the pentecostal movement takes on great significance. There is hardly ever a prayer meeting at which there is no petition on behalf of sick or crippled members and friends. Indeed, among the 155 groups surveyed for this study, the experience of witnessing actual physical healing at a prayer meeting is not uncommon (37%). The members who reported these cures did so from firsthand knowledge, but most of them tend to agree with the man from Alabama who wrote: "Healings from resentments and burdened feelings are both more common and more significant than physical healings." The charismatics' faith in prayer and in the miraculous power of the Lord is accompanied by a deep concern for the ill health, both mental and physical, of their fellow human beings.[27] This, too, must be called a personal involvement in the corporal works of mercy.

The information we have gathered indicates that the members of the movement feel very strongly that the primary charismatic function, the praise and glory of God, must in no way be diminished or set aside. "Human need has been thrust upon them," writes the famous David Wilkerson. "Our calling is not first to addicts, widows, the weak and poor. Our ministry is first and foremost to Christ! We are called first to His praise and glory. To meet His need before we feed the multitudes."[28]

6

Personal Relations among Charismatics

One of the human factors that attract people to membership in the charismatic renewal is the close and friendly relationship that exists within the local prayer group. If human love is exhibited by warm embraces, joyful smiles, friendly greetings, and mutual encouragement, the casual observer at a pentecostal prayer meeting might well exclaim, "These charismatics! See how they love one another!" When the Eucharist is celebrated at the meetings, the members join hands during the recitation of the Lord's Prayer and they exchange the Kiss of Peace in a manner that bespeaks their spiritual solidarity. For contrast, one need merely observe the relatively aloof way in which this ritual is performed at Sunday Mass in many parish churches.

Membership in the charismatic renewal not only makes friends, but also attracts friends. In his study of recruitment to Catholic pentecostalism, Harrison found that three out of five of those who received the baptism of the Spirit in the Ann Arbor community first heard about the movement from close friends. He suggests that merely hearing about the movement from other sources is not nearly so conducive to someone's joining it as learning about it from a friend who is an active and enthusiastic participant.[1] This means of introduction seems more effective than some of the "predisposing factors" investigated by social scientists.

The kind of fellowship exhibited in primary face-to-face relations that is said to characterize the typical Protestant church congregation is now in evidence among Catholic pentecostals. At the prayer meetings the members are on a first-name basis—a familiarity that extends to priests and religious sisters and brothers—and they often wear a first-name tag that invites this intimacy even from strangers. The concept of "sharing" is very popular among them, and they frequently express their willingness to "share" an experience, an idea, a prayer or teaching, or a prophecy. They seem to feel a longing for community, which may account for the popularity of Zablocki's account of the Bruderhof among them.[2]

Growth of Friendship

Although the question of why some Catholics join the charismatic renewal while others do not has been explored in several studies, no definitive explanation has as yet emerged. Theories of deprivation—economic, political, psychological, and religious—which suggest that some significant need is being satisfied by people who join religious movements, remain suggestive rather than demonstrable. One anthropologist believes that membership in a pentecostal group may satisfy a feeling of "affective deprivation." The craving for the kind of affection that is demonstrated among charismatics may lead some people to the prayer group. "Seeking community adds the promise of enduring

friendship, enduring love, and this gives meaning and stability to their existence."[3]

There is no doubt that the quest for community and the
personal need for friendship and affection characterize much
of contemporary society, yet membership in religious movements like Catholic pentecostalism is only one of several
ways in which these needs can be met. Practically everybody
appreciates affective response from fellow human beings,
and Catholic charismatics also show this appreciation. Pentecostal theologians content themselves with saying that
God moves individuals to the renewal, that the Spirit bestows special graces on the members, but they have no
reason for denying that the initial contact is usually with
an enthusiastic member who invites friends to attend prayer
meetings.

Although many of the charismatic prayer groups around
the country include non-Catholics in their membership,[4]
we wished to look at Catholicism as a primary factor of
shared friendship. Indeed, when we asked our respondents
about the religious affiliations of their three closest friends
(excluding spouses), we found that less than three percent
numbered no Catholics among their close friends. We then
asked how many of these close friends attended charismatic
prayer meetings with the respondent. The replies allowed
us to set up and compare four categories: 153 (21%) who are
not accompanied to prayer meetings by a close friend; 165
(22%) who attend with one friend; 192 (26%), with two friends;
and 234 (31%), with three friends.

We made the obvious assumption that prayer groups
themselves foster friendships and then tested the hypothesis
that the longer a person has been in the charismatic renewal,
the more likely he will be to report that he has three close
Catholic friends who attend meetings with him. Among

101

those who are not accompanied by friends, 46% have been in the movement one year or less, as compared with only 18% of those who attend with three close friends. Only 9% of the former, as compared with 35% of the latter, have been in the movement three years or longer. Let us redistribute these statistics more specifically in Table 6.1.

The statistics in Table 6.1 strongly support the generalization that friendships are fostered and multiplied by membership in the charismatic movement. A very large proportion (79%) of those who have been longest in the movement are accompanied to prayer meetings by two or three close friends. Of those who have been the shortest time in the movement, however, the larger proportion (62%) go to the meeting alone or with only one close friend. While there are unquestionably other factors that account for the growth of friendships, the mutual appreciation inspired by the charismatic experience is obviously one of the principal factors.

The most dedicated charismatics are also those who most

TABLE 6.1

Proportions Attending Meetings with Friends According to Length of Time in the Movement

	TIME IN THE MOVEMENT		
Member attends with	% 1 year and less (n = 232)	% 2 or 3 years (n = 410)	% Over 3 years (n = 102)
No close friend	31	19	4
One friend	31	19	17
Two friends	20	28	29
Three friends	18	34	50

enthusiastically encourage their friends to attend prayer meetings. The rapid multiplication of prayer groups in the United States seems to be due more to this personal enthusiasm than to the advertising and propaganda that appear occasionally as inducements to attendance and membership. The growth of the publishing services of the movement is clearly after the fact—that is, after people have joined the movement and participated in its activities, they clamor for more reading and instructional materials. Evangelizing and proselytizing are thus characteristic activities of the movement's most enthusiastic members.[5]

We have seen previously (Table 4.1) that membership in the charismatic renewal tends to foster a greater appreciation for the so-called traditional religious practices of Catholicism. In Table 6.2 we now find another explanation

TABLE 6.2

Proportions Who Perform Religious Practices "More Often"
According to Number of Close Catholic Friends

	% AMONG RESPONDENTS REPORTING 0-3 FRIENDS			
	% No Friends (n = 153)	% One (n = 165)	% Two (n = 192)	% Three (n = 234)
Receiving Holy Communion	67	70	81	85
Attending Holy Mass	66	70	80	85
Visiting the Blessed Sacrament	50	61	64	71
Going to Confession	26	34	35	47
Praying the Rosary	22	26	24	42

for this phenomenon. The person who has close Catholic friends in the movement is also likely to develop this appreciation for traditional Catholic devotions. The statistical difference of response is significant in this regard, and is probably to be expected. A comparison of the first and fourth columns of Table 6.2 reveals that those whose close friends are non-Catholics are less likely to engage in these religious practices than are people who have three close Catholic friends. These findings may be extended beyond the charismatic renewal for they support the larger notion that close association with one's fellow religionists has an important influence on one's own religious practices. We do not have research data from the ecumenical prayer groups in which the majority of members are non-Catholics, but we can safely hypothesize that the Catholics in such groups have a lower record of participation in traditional religious practices.

There are two other pieces of evidence concerning differential attachment to Catholicism. The first is that those with no close Catholic friends are more likely (29% to 19%) to say that the charismatic renewal does not really need the clergy because the Holy Spirit bestows His charisms on the laity. The second is that they are more willing (57% to 38%) to ignore the orders of a bishop who would forbid charismatic prayer meetings in his diocese.

Sex and Marital Status

One of the interesting facts about the charismatics who are not accompanied to prayer meetings by any close friend is that two-thirds (65%) of them are men. We know that at prayer meetings, conferences, and conventions of Catholic pentecostalism there are always more females than males present.[6] The preponderance of females—roughly about

104

two-thirds of those in attendance—seems easily explained by the fact that a woman charismatic is more likely than a man to bring a friend along.

Another interesting point is that those who bring no friend to the prayer meetings are more likely (88%) to be married than are those who have three close friends at meetings (79%). Further, a comparative analysis of the data concerning sex and marital status indicates that while married men usually attend meetings with their wives, some married women may come with friends rather than with their husbands. Although we have no accurate statistics on this matter, it seems safe to say that married women are more likely than married men to come to prayer meetings without their spouses.

Priest-leaders often advise against this practice. They try to persuade married women, especially those whose husbands are not attracted to pentecostalism, to stay at home with their husbands and families. There are numerous opportunities in large cities for women to participate in daytime prayer meetings conducted by exclusively female groups. Sue Manney discusses this problem with complete frankness: "Sometimes, the spouse is simply not interested in spiritual growth at this point in his life. He views this sudden talk on spiritual matters as an unnecessary intrusion in a marriage he feels is fine without it, or it is seen as a threat to an already difficult marital relationship." She suggests that the married woman who goes to an evening prayer meeting without her husband should ask herself: "Am I leaving behind a home where the Lord's peace would be evident to anyone stopping by tonight? If you can't say yes to the last question, you don't belong at the prayer meeting on that particular night. You belong at home."[7]

Among the unmarried respondents to this survey, there

105

is a small proportion (12%) who have no close Catholic friends in the charismatic renewal. The percentage of these friendless charismatics is smaller among single women (8%) than among single men (18%) which is an indication not only of greater religiosity among women, but also of their willingness to seek out companions who will go with them to prayer meetings.

The "total commitment" that is demanded of members in Communist cells, Catholic religious orders, and some idealistic communes is alien to the charismatic renewal, which sees itself as an instrument for helping people to lead better family lives and to perform effectively their occupational and other social roles.[8] Even those who tend to withdraw from the world to form covenant communities do not insist on the biblical dictum, "Leave father and mother for My name's sake." The regeneration that comes with baptism in the Spirit does not imply a competition with other institutions for the member's loyalty. It does mean, however, that every facet of human living must, for the charismatic member, be inspired by the Lord and carried on in obedience to the divine will. This is why there is constant reference to "discernment" and a dedication to petitionary prayer even when the local groups are dealing with mundane matters.

There are many who witness to the beneficent influence that the charismatic experience has had on their personal relations. A twenty-nine-year-old college instructor from Rhode Island writes that "the charismatic renewal has answered a need in my life for a deeper sense of community with my brothers and sisters. My husband has also begun attending prayer meetings, and this has deepened our ability to relate to one another and to express love with our young children." A thirty-six-year-old professional man from

New Mexico talks similarly of better family relations: "Being in the charismatic renewal has helped me be a better husband, father and neighbor. It has helped me to find Christ in my own life and to recognize His spirit in everybody around me."

Nevertheless, the charismatic renewal has in many instances functioned as a source of disunity and even of rancor in the family. Younger people who enthusiastically embrace pentecostalism frequently find their parents in strong opposition, a typical example of the "generation gap" in reverse. Parents who are ordinarily concerned about the immorality of youth are replaced by parents who feel that their children are getting "too religious" when they want to participate in the charismatic prayer meetings. Some mothers have even put restrictions on their teen-age daughters, forbidding them to attend prayer meetings more than once a month.

A more common pattern is that in which the charismatic renewal causes frustration between husband and wife. It is most often the woman who not only experiences a deeper religious and devotional life in the movement, but also finds a new depth of friendship among the members of the group. Her enthusiasm directs her love away from her husband and children and toward her fellow charismatics, with whom she has developed a satisfying spiritual relationship. The mixed marriage of a Catholic and a non-Catholic may produce certain problems, but these have usually been anticipated. The mixed marriage of a charismatic and a non-charismatic is much more difficult in that the baptism of the Spirit produces unexpected changes in the attitudes and behavior of the charismatic spouse. As one husband remarked, "She's much harder to live with since she got religion."

Role and Status of Women

Although females far outnumber males in the charismatic renewal, they are being taught by the theoreticians of the movement to be submissive to male authority.[9] Even the women themselves seem to accept this subordination as the will of God. Sue Manney writes that "God created man to be the head of woman, and he created woman to be in submission to the man. . . . No matter how deep her insight may be, a woman must be in submission to her husband just as Christ is submissive to the Father, perfectly obedient in all things. . . . When a woman submits to her husband and acknowledges his headship, she is submitting to the will of God."[10]

In light of this ideology, it is not surprising to find that only three out of ten (29%) of our respondents agree that the Catholic Church should take a stand in support of the Women's Liberation Movement, and that only one-third of them favor the ordination of women to the Catholic priesthood. It may be surprising, however, to learn that women play a "principal" role in 45% of the 155 prayer groups from which we collected research data. One sister in Ohio said that she takes a principal role in the group "only because there are no strong men to assume the role." A laywoman from Indiana says that because of her own experience as a principal leader, she helped bring about "a formal decision that there be no women on the pastoral team." It appears, then, that most charismatic women want men to assume the leadership and that it is only by default that they are willing to do so themselves.

This submissive stance does not mean that women are merely passive participants in the charismatic renewal. We have observed that at the actual prayer meetings women express themselves more often than men in witness, in prophecy, in spontaneous quotation from scripture, and in other paraliturgical ways. The Word of God Community at Ann Arbor officially designates some women as "handmaids" (deaconesses), and these women "have a good deal of responsibility for the spiritual growth of the women of the community."[11] From the organizational point of view, many "ministries of service" are performed mainly by women: they take care of altar linens, provide refreshments, befriend newcomers, pray with individuals for special intentions, visit sick members, and baby-sit on days of renewal. Perhaps women have always and everywhere performed such services more willingly and competently than men, but these are obviously not the functions of leadership.

The first knowledge I had of the Catholic pentecostal movement came from a woman reporter, Mary Papa, who wrote an eyewitness account of "People Having a Good Time Praying."[12] This story so impressed the pioneer renewalists Kevin and Dorothy Ranaghan that they used excerpts from it to head each chapter of their book *Catholic Pentecostals*. This book shows that women were "bearing witness" from the start—three of them telling of their charismatic conversion at Duquesne University, and three others later at Notre Dame University.[13] Most of the early leaders and authors, however, were men.

Dorothy Ranaghan continued to carry the message of renewal by contributing two chapters to another book, *As the Spirit Leads Us,* which she coedited with her husband.[14] Susan B. Anthony also added a chapter to that work, and Virginia Kortenkamp cooperated with her husband Leon in providing another chapter. Further, one of the most thoughtful commentators on the movement is a female theologian, Professor J. Massingberd Ford, whose small monograph, *The Pentecostal Experience,* is a model of corrective enthusiasm.[15]

Beyond these few examples, however, one has to search

widely and diligently for the published words of charismatic spokeswomen. The content of *New Covenant,* which is properly considered a "teaching" instrument of the movement, is provided almost exclusively by men. The editor is Ralph Martin and the monthly feature, "Your Word," is regularly written by George Martin. Volume II (July 1972 to June 1973) contained eighty-seven feature articles with writers' bylines. Seventy-seven of them were written by men; two, by religious sisters; four, by laywomen; and four, jointly by married couples. These figures indicate that writing functions hardly at all as a teaching role for women in the movement's national periodical.

Let us look away from the publication office at Ann Arbor and toward Notre Dame, where the members of True House prayer community had the burden of conducting the International Conference of the Charismatic Renewal in 1973. There were probably many unsung women volunteers who worked hard in preparation for this conference, busying themselves with many aspects of the program itself—I saw them there. Yet the steering committee was made up of seven men and only two women, while the official conference staff was comprised of ten males (one a priest) and two females (one a sister). Here again, with these few exceptions, women played subsidiary roles.

Nevertheless, the spiritual benefits of the renewal movement continue to attract increasing numbers of American Catholic women to participation in group prayer. This is particularly noticeable in the proliferation of exclusively female groups which meet in the homes of various members during the daytime.[16] The women who initiate these groups and invite their friends to attend have, for the most part, been trained in Life-in-the-Spirit and Growth-in-the-Spirit seminars. There is no reason to suppose that they are less

110

graced with the charisms of the Spirit or less competent than males to promote the prayer patterns of the pentecostal movement.

Piety and religiosity are still more characteristic of women than of men in western society, and this is true among Catholic pentecostals. When we compared the responses of the men and women who answered our questionnaires, we found that all had been baptized in the Spirit and that all read the Scriptures frequently. Yet there were the expected sex differences in beliefs and practices: for example, women are more likely than men to affirm that they speak in tongues, that the Second Coming of Christ is imminent, that accepting Jesus means that they are saved, and that they now attend Mass and receive Communion more often than they used to. Thus, the charismatic renewal has provided a further outlet for their religiosity.

Clergy-Lay Relations

The American beginnings of the Catholic pentecostal movement can be traced to the lay people who conducted the first discussions and prayer meetings without benefit of Catholic clergy.[17] This does not suggest that the charismatic renewal was ever considered or intended to be a movement exclusively for the Catholic laity.[18] Indeed, Catholic priests soon became aware of it and began to involve themselves in it in ever-increasing numbers. Yet Edward O'Connor has remarked that "some people imagine that if a person is being guided by the Holy Spirit he has no need of the ordinary human guidance that comes through the pastoral office of the Church."[19]

It is a well-known fact that some of the lower-class Protestant pentecostal groups have little use for ordained ministers. They repudiate sacramentalism and sacerdotalism and

111

are often anticlerical in their attitudes toward the Catholic priesthood. Because they enjoy the charismatic gifts of the Holy Spirit, they feel no religious need for an official priesthood. In an attempt to discover whether this anticlerical attitude had invaded the Catholic renewal, we included the following statement in our survey questionnaire: "Since lay people receive the gifts of the Spirit, the charismatic renewal could go on without the clergy." Three-quarters (76%) of the respondents disagreed with this position, leaving only a small minority who felt they could get along without priests.

George Martin argues that the charismatic renewal brings a closer relationship between laity and clergy and bridges the gap between the "neat categories" that existed before Vatican II. "It is clear that the charismatic ministries do not replace the ordained ministry; priests need not worry about becoming obsolete. Rather, just the opposite seems to be occurring." The movement holds the promise of fuller involvement of everybody in the Church "because its primary focus is not on the differences between clergy and laity, but on the gifts of service that every follower of Christ receives."[20]

Lay people unquestionably continue to exercise leadership among the local prayer groups, however, and in some instances they exert greater influence than does the clergy.[21] We know from the official *Directory* of charismatic groups that many lay persons, as well as religious sisters and brothers, are listed as "contact persons" for local prayer groups.[22] We have no comparative information about the "leadership qualities" of these people, but we assume that they are at least spokesmen for, or representatives of, their groups, and we also assume that they can perform these functions as well as clergymen.

Whether or not it is essential to the organized movement

112

that the designated leader be a priest, it is obvious that a priest must be at hand for those weekly prayer meetings which conclude with the celebration of the Eucharist. Thus, it does seem to us an indication of a "shortage" of clergy when four out of ten (39%) of the groups report that they do not have a priest-leader regularly in attendance at their weekly prayer meetings. One respondent from Michigan remarked harshly that "priests in this area do not want to get involved with the movement because they treat their commitment to God as a job—done at 5:00 P.M. They do not live a life in the Spirit." Another person, from Delaware, laid down the dictum that "all clergy should have baptism in the Holy Spirit. Unless they are Spirit-filled, I don't see how they can aid people with deep spiritual problems."

There is another aspect of the clergy's participation in the charismatic renewal that is much more personal to the priest himself. This is the question of the religious, spiritual, and vocational effects that the charismatic experience has on priests. Our hypothesis, of course, is that this is a conversion experience that affects everyone who undergoes it, priests as well as laity, and brings the individual closer to God and the Church. Almost every issue of *New Covenant* provides proof of this generalization in the form of personal witness of the beneficial changes that have occurred in the lives of the priest-authors.[23]

The notion that membership in the charismatic renewal implies a deeply spiritual conversion does not mean that the movement provides a therapeutic nostrum for all the personal problems that may plague the man of God. Bishop McKinney writes that "while many priests find the answer to their own struggle in moments of faith-crisis within the charismatic renewal, they should not play a leadership role until they have integrated their personal faith life and their

113

role as leader of the faith community. A priest with 'hang-ups' can cause great harm if he imposes them on the prayer community."[24]

At the very beginning of the survey, we were alerted to the fact that several well-known charismatic priest-leaders had left the movement and the priesthood. On the original list of contact persons taken from the 1972 *Directory*, we had to replace the names of five priests to whom we had sent postcards of enquiry. One responded quite frankly, "I am no longer a member of the Roman Church." Three were on "leave of absence" from their religious order and have since departed the priesthood. Another was a prominent national leader who had conducted the only officially established Catholic pentecostal parish in the United States, and who felt that he was not giving up the ministry when he threw in his lot with Protestant pentecostals.[25] Information of this kind represented an unexpected intrusion into the glowing picture that is everywhere drawn of the charismatic clergy, but we were reminded of O'Connor's remark: "There have even been several instances of priests and nuns who left the Church on the ground that they had found the true life in the Spirit elsewhere."[26]

Despite these and other relatively negative reports of clerical defection, the large majority of lay charismatics see the clerical role as essential to the movement. One woman from California wrote: "We don't really have pastoral guidance of the charismatic renewal in our area. I wish there was a team of charismatic priests and lay people traveling about the country to speak in the Catholic churches and visit our individual prayer meetings. We have had some Catholics getting re-baptized in other churches and some have left our Church."

Here, then, we return to the idea of a cooperative relationship between laity and clergy and to the basic question of whether there is a shortage of priests in the movement, for the fact is that some people are leaving the Catholic Church for want of pastoral guidance. A thirty-nine-year-old secretary from Illinois writes that "we need the spiritual direction of a Spirit-filled priest. I am greatly concerned that many Spirit-filled lay people are leaving the Church because of a lack of Spirit-filled guidance by priests." In a similar vein a businessman from New Mexico observes that "many members of the Church are seeking for a deeper knowledge of Jesus Christ and are looking elsewhere because our priests do not preach the Gospel." In the light of all this evidence, one may conclude that the pentecostal movement is growing so fast among lay Catholics that the supply of properly trained priests cannot keep up with it.[27]

Relations with the Hierarchy

One of the triumphant moments of the charismatic renewal came in October 1973, when international leaders met for a conference in Rome and thirteen of them had a brief private audience with Paul VI. The prepared text of the Pope's greeting to them did not specifically mention the Catholic pentecostal movement, but it did emphasize that "the spiritual lives of the faithful, therefore, come under the active pastoral responsibility of each bishop in his own diocese." The Pope warned that "weeds" may be found among the good seed. "So a work of discernment is indispensable; it devolves upon those who are in charge of the Church."[28]

The Holy Father left no doubt that any Catholic movement of renewal must remain firmly under the episcopal control of the Church. At the Notre Dame conference in June 1973, the keynote speaker, Father Cohen, "called on Pope Paul VI to exercise discernment about the true nature

115

and proper use of the charismatic gifts."[29] In the name of the movement he addressed the bishops: "We need your discernment. We pledge you our obedience. I would drop every charismatic activity in New Orleans tomorrow if my bishop told me to do so."[30]

This pledge of absolute loyalty to the hierarchy is not acceptable to all members of the charismatic renewal. Paul de Celles, one of the original lay leaders of the movement (now a deacon), took issue "with the notion that we should automatically obey a bishop who asks us to stop participation in the Catholic charismatic renewal." He pointed out that there is strong participation by the laity in many areas where the clergy is not interested. This is a "new type of emerging ministry, a new type of broad spectrum of service." Furthermore, the emphasis on clerical and episcopal presence at charismatic assemblies and the insistence on obedience to the bishops and the Pope are "indicative of a trend toward a clericalism which does not reflect the Spirit-led attitude of thousands of people in the charismatic renewal."[31]

That de Celles is speaking for a large number of lay charismatics is confirmed by the fact that 45% of our respondents would continue to hold prayer meetings even if the bishop of their diocese issued a prohibition against it. A convert, a fifty-seven-year-old male from Northern New York, asks, "How could a bishop prohibit people from having prayer meetings in their homes?" A thirty-seven-year-old woman from South Dakota said that she would obey the bishop "because he is appointed by God. I don't believe God would allow the bishop to prohibit these meetings unless He were somehow going to use the results for His greater honor and glory."

In the early days of the prayer group at Notre Dame, Bishop Pursley ordered priests to withdraw from active leadership in the charismatic movement, whereupon the suggestion was made that the meetings be canceled. The group voted on this proposal and rejected it, "declaring that the Pentecostal movement was not dependent on clerical direction, but had developed chiefly under lay leadership."[32] Among the lay respondents to this survey, only a small minority (24%) agreed that the charismatic renewal is not dependent on the Catholic clergy and could go on without them. The dissenters are also less willing than the rest (58% to 82%) to accept Pope Paul VI as the infallible Vicar of Christ, and they are more in favor than the others (44% to 33%) of the popular election of bishops.

We do not know to what extent charismatic prayer groups, and their priest-leaders, may be having "trouble" with the bishops and their chancery officials. In 1969 the National Conference of Catholic Bishops received from its Committee on Doctrine a lukewarm and cautious report on the Catholic pentecostal movement which said that "the reaction to this movement seems to be one of caution and somewhat unhappy." The Committee recommended that the "bishops keep in mind their pastoral responsibility to oversee and guide this movement in the Church."[33] With this in mind we asked the leaders about their diocesan bishop's attitude toward the prayer groups. In the eighty-eight dioceses covered in our survey, there were forty-three bishops who gave full approval to the charismatic renewal. Most of the others merely "tolerated" it.

There are some bishops who were once suspicious, or even antagonistic, but who have now come to accept the prayer groups. One respondent wrote that "when we first began the bishop told our pastor that he could not attend prayer meetings and that we had to move from parish facilities. We all obeyed with no bitterness. Now there are many

117

prayer meetings in the diocese and the bishop has appointed a monsignor as official liaison between the hierarchy and the charismatic renewal." Not all bishops, however, have experienced this change of heart. Another person remarked that "the bishop of this diocese discourages people from attending charismatic meetings, but he does not forbid them to attend. Because of this no priests from our parish come to the meetings, but we have invited them on many occasions."

Remarks of this kind from lay people at the "grass roots" of the movement led me to make inquiries of Bishop Joseph McKinney, the episcopal moderator of the American charismatic movement. He said that about ninety percent of the bishops he contacted showed "cautious approval." He said also that "many bishops have made it a point to appoint a diocesan moderator to keep in touch with a priest who is involved. Many would like to issue guidelines but there are so many different expressions of the movement that it does not seem to be opportune for them at this time."[34]

While the Catholic pentecostals want the approval of the hierarchy, they do not want episcopal control. While they want good relations between the clergy and the laity, they resist clericalism. While they desire close personal friendships among the membership, they want to admit as little structure and organization as possible. A theoretical consistency characterizes the whole area of human relations in the Catholic charismatic renewal—the belief that they must neither hamper nor attempt to structure the spontaneous ways of behaving of people who are completely open to the influence of the Holy Spirit.

The fact that the above generalizations emerge from statistical majorities of the respondents must not blind us to some of the "trouble spots" in the charismatic renewal. There is no doubt that the bonds of love and friendship are strengthened among the majority of Catholic pentecostals, but despite the movement's efforts to limit controversy, conflict, and dissent, there are people, both lay and clerical, who drop out. In the practical order of human relations, there remain certain "minority problems" that show up in the survey statistics. Few black Catholics are attracted to the movement; not all female members are content with the subordinate position to which they have been assigned; and not all lay members accept the guidance, much less leadership, of the clergy. Ford tells us that no priest (or woman) is permitted to lead a prayer meeting of the South Bend People of Praise charismatics. Further, the notion that episcopal approval is desirable for the movement remains questionable for a significant minority of the membership. In other words, the special charisms of the movement still leave the members to cope humanly with everyday social relations.[35]

7

Prophets, Miracles, and Demons

Catholic pentecostals firmly believe that they are in contact with the divine, that God has "touched" them, that they have a special relationship with the Holy Spirit, and that God reveals Himself to them either personally or through group discernment. This kind of sacred relationship between God and human beings escapes the analytical tools of the empirical social scientist and is merely analogous to the kinds of social interaction that can be empirically studied.[1] Nevertheless, charismatic people are convinced that this relationship is operative in their own lives, and their observable religious behavior is based on this conviction. To discount it, or ignore it, would be to write off the whole pentecostal movement as an ephemeral phenomenon.

This transcendental relationship is manifest to the members of the movement in the charismatic title by which they identify themselves. By virtue of the Spirit-baptism, they feel themselves to be in possession of some or all of the charisms that came upon Christ's followers at the original

Pentecost. Our sociological survey of the lay participants reveals that several principal areas of this charismatic relationship center on the prophetic and healing ministries. In this chapter we shall attempt to analyze the research data concerning these phenomena.

Prophecy as Message

In the Judaic-Christian tradition the prophet or prophetess is a channel of communication from God to human beings. It is the belief of Catholics that divine *self*-communication was closed with the God-man, Jesus Christ. Nevertheless, human prophets "still have their para-institutional place in the Church because ever and again there are people in the Church divinely sent to it to bear a personal testimony to the reality of God and Christ in the might of his Spirit."[2] In this sense the person who prophesies is delivering a message from God. This is a charismatic ability that Paul recognized among some of the early Christians and saw as distinct from other gifts of the Spirit.

Anyone who has regularly attended charismatic prayer meetings has heard these prophetic communications, usually spoken with apparent spontaneity, and more often by women than by men. After a while one recognizes a pattern of thematic statements such as, "I am your Father who loves you, and I ask only that you love me with all your heart." This model is similar to that of the approved prophecy delivered at the International Charismatic Conference: "I am the Lord, I am present with you here. I am the Lord, and I have chosen now to act. I will awake this world to hear my voice. I will awake this world to hear the voice of its Lord, the mighty King. And I will speak my words of everlasting love to the hearts of men."[3]

A second example of "God's Word to Us," also spoken

121

at the Conference, begins as follows: "Oh my beloved children, if you knew the love that I am pouring forth in the deepest part of your being, if you but understood the gentleness of my love, the tenderness of the Shepherd's heart, would you not open up to me this night to receive the love that I freely give to you? For in this very hour I am among you to love you with a love that shall consume you." While expressions of this kind are very common at charismatic prayer meetings and can be made by anyone present, there are certain people who come to be recognized by the members as specially gifted with the prophetic charism. I have interviewed three recognized prophetesses, each of whom said modestly that she was unworthy of such a title and that she had no rational explanation for the fact that "God speaks" through her.

The typical skeptical scientist is not alone in questioning the authenticity of the prophetic person and the prophetic message. Gelpi warns that "although the true gift of prophecy must be held in esteem by all Christians, the value of any given prophecy, as in the case of other charismatic movements, must be tested reflectively by the community in union with its official leaders."[4] He makes the point that while the individual is privileged in possessing this gift, the prophetic charism entails a message brought from "outside" him or her for the benefit of the prayer group. Therefore, the honor bestowed on the prophetic person is not nearly so important as the divine message delivered to the faithful.

Leaders of the charismatic renewal have attempted to analyze the prophetic function, to distinguish between true and false prophecy, and to separate these from "nonprophecy," which is simply the personal thought of an individual "dressed up in prophetic form." Bruce Yocum, a coordinator of the Word of God Community in Ann Arbor, says that he has himself uttered prophecies and remarks that "just as a good teacher prepares his classes, a good prophet will make himself ready to hear the Lord."[5] The prophet is said to receive a spontaneous impulse from God to deliver a message, but one gets the impression that it is possible to "learn how" to be a prophet in the pentecostal movement.

The prospective prophet "must exercise responsibility by learning to speak the Lord's word faithfully." Careful instructions are provided by Yocum concerning the content of the prophetic message, the place and time, manner and form for it, and the language with which it should be announced. It must be done in an orderly way at the prayer meeting. The "guidelines" for testing prophecy require this controlled orderliness because "occasionally someone will decide that his personal criticisms of the leadership in a prayer group, of his church, or of a person with whom he is having a dispute will carry more weight if they are given as prophecy." Discord of this kind and personal motivation fail the test of true prophecy. God does not "thunder" in anger at these charismatic people; He does not become "upset" with them. He speaks only in positive terms of love and encouragement. "No true prophecy will reveal a God who is vindictive, harsh or cruel."[6]

For Catholic charismatics the ultimate norm for the testing of true divine messages appears to be the "rule of faith." From a negative point of view, this means that any utterance contradictory to the doctrines of the Catholic Church is immediately suspect as a false communication. On more than one occasion a large charismatic group in New Orleans was "invaded" by Protestant pentecostals who proclaimed prophecies that denigrated the Virgin Mary, the Catholic hierarchy, and the sacramental system of the

123

Church. Their message was drowned out by the assembled guitarists while they were politely ushered to the exit.

Most messages by people with the prophetic gift are delivered in the vernacular, but they are also occasionally hidden under the cover of glossolalia. The great majority (86%) of our respondents say that they have received the charism of speaking in tongues, but very few of them claim to have been given the gift of prophecy. It appears, then, that the "interpretation" of the divine message is the function of the prophetic person. Most people who speak or sing in tongues say that this is simply a form of praise and worship of God which they do not pretend to interpret. Paul, however, "speaks of instances of glossolalia in which the tongue is interpreted not by the one who speaks but by a second party who understands the meaning that is hidden from the speaker himself."[7]

In some cases wherein the "interpretation" of glossolalia is made by a second party, it is believed that the Lord is sending a message through the person who speaks in tongues. It is interesting that John Sherrill, who is greatly revered by Catholic pentecostals, presents numerous cases of people who spoke in languages they did not know— Arabic, German, Polish, Hebrew, Swedish, and others. When he submitted about forty tape recordings of these tongue experiences to language experts, however, no real or known language was recognized by any of them.[8] Most Catholic charismatics who are willing to accept an interpretive divine communication through the gift of tongues do not accept Sherrill's stories about tongues in strange languages unknown to the speaker.[9]

Prophecy as Prediction

It is probably no exaggeration to say that most people think of a prophet as a person who foretells the future. As

124

Yocum remarks, "A very traditional test of genuine prophecy is whether or not the word spoken, if the prophecy is a prediction, comes to pass as the prophet said it would." J. Massingberd Ford, however, like most theological commentators on the Catholic charismatic movement, says that "it is important to realize that prophecy does not necessarily imply prediction."[10] She adds that in all of her experience in the movement, she knows of no specific prediction given at a prayer meeting of Catholics.[11] One may here recall Kilian McDonnell's account of the young widower who was approached by a woman with the claim that the Holy Spirit had revealed to her in prophecy that they were to marry. When he told her that another woman had received the same prophecy, she replied that the first lady was a "false prophet."[12]

Aside from such frivolous incidents, the charismatic Christian may be forgiven for thinking in terms of predictive prophecy. After all, the Old Testament prophets are best remembered by modern Christians as having foretold the coming of the Messiah. Large numbers of contemporary Catholic pentecostals firmly believe that the Second Coming of Christ is imminent. This expectation seems to be based on a borrowing from classical Protestant pentecostalism rather than on a specific prophecy delivered to a Catholic prayer group.[13] One of the favorites among the Old Testament prophets is Ezekial, whose prediction concerning the "dry bones" in the midst of the valley is often quoted by Catholic charismatics. More than one prayer group has called itself "Ezekial 37" as a reminder that God has imbued its members with new life.

A prophecy that rocked the Catholic charismatic community was pronounced in August 1973 by the venerated author of *The Cross and the Switchblade,* David Wilkerson. This hero of the movement fell from grace when he revealed that "the clearest vision" he had ever received from God predicted an era of intense persecution for all Spirit-filled Christians. "He predicted that the warm reception Catholic charismatics are receiving in the Catholic Church will not continue and that both Catholic and Protestant charismatics will be forced to leave their churches and form a 'supernatural church of true believers.' "[14]

This negative prophecy could not go unchallenged by Catholic leaders of the renewal. It went directly counter to the pentecostal vision within the Catholic Church as well as to the ecumenical aspirations of the main-line Christian churches. Ralph Martin charged Wilkerson with "sensationalism," a spirit of self-justification, and an independent unwillingness to submit his vision to the scrutiny of others. Martin is sure that Wilkerson is "not hearing the Lord correctly here," and that he is demonstrating "traditional pentecostal prejudice, even hostility, to the established churches."[15]

David du Plessis, a venerable veteran among the classical Protestant pentecostals, came to the support of his Catholic friends. He said that he had been hearing these kinds of predictions for more than fifty years and that he knows all about the "false prophets who spoke out of pure prejudice and hatred."[16] While he is deeply grieved by the prophecy of his "good brother David Wilkerson," he is convinced that John XXIII, Vatican II, and Paul VI have moved the Catholic Church in the right pentecostal direction. Wilkerson's vision has been the subject of discussion and discernment in prayer groups all over the country, and their repudiation of it seems to derive mainly from the fact that it was a one-man prophecy and not subject to the scrutiny of the proper charismatic authorities.

If there is a scientific way to "test" the truth of a prophetic prediction, it lies only in awaiting the eventual outcome of the forecast. If, in fact, Pope Paul or one of his successors should pronounce a condemnation of the Catholic charismatic movement, this scientific test would be met and we would then have to admit that David Wilkerson had accurately foretold the event. No amount of consultation by the movement or its official leaders—either now or in the future— could contravene such evidence. No scientific approach, however, can answer the question of whether this gloomy prophecy came from God, from the devil, or from neither. Martin is convinced that "the devil is certainly trying to prevent the remarkable renewal that is going on."[17] It is entirely possible for a prophecy inspired neither by God nor the devil to be fulfilled by chance.

The Miracle of Healing

The belief that God can and sometimes does cure people who have not been benefited by medical procedures is traditional among Catholics and has been confirmed by experiences at such places as Lourdes and Fatima.[18] This faith has apparently been widely renewed among the members of the pentecostal movement. "God has healed his people before. But now he is doing it in a way that no one remembers having seen. . . . There will always be situations in which reasonable men can express reasonable doubts, but the evidence is rapidly becoming overwhelming that most of the reports of healing are authentic beyond question."[19]

In order to clarify the evidence and to exclude "hearsay" testimony, we asked the leaders of the 155 prayer groups covered in our national survey: "Have you been personally present at a Prayer Meeting at which the gift of healing was granted by the Lord?" Then we asked that they briefly

127

describe "what happened." In fifty-seven of these groups (37%), there had occurred the healing of physical infirmities; in thirty-nine groups (25%), there were reports of various kinds of spiritual and psychological healings. The remaining groups had experienced no miraculous cures of any type.

One of the frequently repeated phrases that is relatively new to Catholic discourse is "healing of the memories," and many of our respondents refer to this as a special grace they have received. In a sense it represents a cleansing of subconscious feelings of anxiety, fear, and worthlessness that prevent people from enjoying life. Professor Ford connects this with the sacrament of penance, "which can do more than heal present sins."[20] Agnes Sanford seems to have discovered it when, although of Scotch Presbyterian ancestry, she actually went to confession to a Catholic priest. Coming from this experience, she said, "I knew by the inner warmth and tingling that my nerves and glands were being healed of their overstrain and weakness. And indeed a healing process did begin in me at that time."[21]

The healing of memories seems to be closely related to the whole conversion process experienced by the pentecostal Catholic. It is so widespread and expected an occurrence that we have not included it within our statistical categories. A leader from Alabama writes that he finds "healing from resentments and burdened feelings to be both more common and more significant than physical healings." A woman from Maryland observes that "some people have had terrible experiences in childhood, but after being prayed over these thoughts and memories no longer plague them." Francis MacNutt remarks that "inner healing is indicated whenever we become aware that we are held down in any way by the hurts of the past. We all suffer from this kind of bondage to one degree or other; some severely, some minimally."[22]

Some of the respondents to this study have given testimony about their own experiences of healing. The mother of a large family in Illinois reveals that for five years she had been under a physician's care for mental depression and exhaustion and was not being cured: "I asked Jesus for help, received the Holy Spirit and in three days was completely cured. That was months before I heard about the charismatic renewal." Another kind of healing occurred for an Indiana businesswoman: "I was an agnostic for six years, a humanistic activist. Now the knowledge of Christ's real, personal saving love for me has given me a real new birth. I am still learning to be a good Catholic and a better Christian."

A dramatic cure of alcoholism is described by a midwestern schoolteacher, who reports: "God cured me of my alcoholism when I received the baptism of the Holy Spirit. Drinking caused me to lose my job, and be out of work for a year. I was about to commit suicide. Psychiatric help and A.A. could not stop me from drinking, but the Holy Spirit did it in the blinking of an eye." Similar confessions were made at some of the prayer meetings we attended: a college student who had broken the marijuana habit, a young woman who had overcome a more serious addiction to heroin after receiving the baptism of the Spirit.

Aside from these spiritual and psychological healings, there is testimony also concerning physical healings that have occurred at the charismatic prayer meetings. Some of these involved the curing of allergies, headaches, sore throats, and back pains; others had to do with arthritic conditions, heart trouble, blindness, and deafness. Even more dramatic instances are related, however. A registered nurse in California reports: "I took care of one man who had massive brain injury from an auto accident. These patients almost always die. We prayed over him and he is now well."

Some respondents were willing to produce evidence in the form of x-rays and confirmation from physicians and surgeons that unusual cures had taken place. A prayer-group leader from Arizona reported on "two cancer healings in which the persons being prayed over felt a great sense of peace and warmth, and these healings were later confirmed by physician's examinations which revealed no evidence of cancer. There was also an ulcer healing confirmed by x-ray following the reception of the Eucharist." From a Michigan prayer group comes the story of a Baptist lady who "was cured of cancer of the mouth, throat and lips," and who sang "Amazing Grace" on her way home, all the way to Toledo. In all, sixteen of the prayer groups in the survey reported the healing of cancer cases.

The most frequently mentioned miracle of physical healing is that of the lengthening of legs. A group leader from Pennsylvania reported that she had actually seen the growth of a leg by two inches and said that "medical history and x-rays are available on this case." Another leader, from a group in Ohio, reported that there had been "many visible lengthenings of legs." People who had worn specially constructed shoes were able to discard them and to return to the use of normal footwear. Those who had witnessed these dramatic cures were impressed by the physical evidence of the miracles.

The petition to God for miraculous intervention in one form or other—the prayer for healing—is most often voiced in separate prayer sessions which occur after the regular group meetings. There remains the fact that in about four out of ten (38%) of the charismatic groups surveyed, there had been no instance of physical healing. In comparing these groups with those in which the healing petition had been answered, we could find no significant differences.

130

Perhaps the rough statistics of a mailed questionnaire survey cannot adequately reveal such differences. The people and the leaders who participate in the privileged prayer groups seem to be quite similar to those in the less privileged. The question arises: Why do miracles happen for some people and not for others?

The puzzling aspect of this question is that the charisms of the Holy Spirit are said to be permanent gifts to the pentecostal person and are not perceived as something that can be "turned on and off." The believer does not question the power of God to heal sickness. He firmly believes that the person who asks in the name of Jesus for a healing, either for himself or for others, can obtain the answer to his petition. To believe that God can heal is not the same as to possess the charism of healing. In the language of the charismatic renewal, the pentecostal Catholic receives the charism of healing through the baptism of the Holy Spirit, and this means that God's healing power is available to him whether or not he becomes a recognized minister of healing.

Catholic pentecostals are slow to use the term "miracle-worker" to describe people who appear to possess the charism of healing others. They are ecumenical enough to hold in admiration well-known Protestant healers like Kathryn Kuhlman, Oral Roberts, and Agnes Sanford, whose books and articles circulate freely among them. A special series of articles on healing, which began in the November 1973 issue of *New Covenant*, featured also the best known Catholic practitioners of the ministry of healing: Mike Scanlon, Barbara Schlemon, and Francis MacNutt. Their popularity is increasing, and they receive more and more invitations to minister to prayer groups all over the country. Yet there is this sober statement from Donald Gelpi: "Roman Catholics tend to approach the faith-healer with immense

131

suspicion and skepticism. They suspect trickery as a way of luring the faithful into the errors of enthusiasm."[23]

While it would be presumptuous to suggest that the art of divine healing can be learned in the way a physician learns the art of medical healing, it seems clear that the Catholic charismatic ministers of healing have modeled themselves after the Protestant faith healers—especially Agnes Sanford and Kathryn Kuhlman. None of them claims to be more than an instrument in the hands of the Lord, but all of them insist that both the healer and the sick person must have complete faith in God before a miraculous cure can be anticipated. Beyond this simple, but profound, generalization there appears to be no answer to the question of whether or not one can "prepare" oneself for healing, either as the healer or as the person to be healed.[24]

The Deliverance Ministry

People who participate in the Catholic pentecostal movement may experience several types of healing: the first is the conversion event itself, which intensifies the repentance for sin; the second is the inner healing of memories, which helps to resolve emotional problems; the third is the actual curing of physical illness and ailments. Beyond these three, however, is the ministry of healing to those who suffer from demonic oppression. Francis MacNutt points out that in the sacramental churches deliverance from the devil takes place in the rite of exorcism.[25]

Concern about the presence and power of evil spirits seems to have developed among Catholic charismatics only after the renewal movement had been in existence for several years. This concern may also be traced, at least in part, to the influence of the pentecostal Protestants. Some charismatic priest-leaders publicly and flatly deny the existence of the devil in the contemporary world. Others are becoming deeply absorbed in tracts like Michael Harper's *Spiritual Warfare*, which describes the tactics to be used in attacking the diabolic enemy.[26] There is now a much greater pre-occupation with this phenomenon than there was when the movement began in 1967.

At the International Charismatic Conference, a lay candidate for the diaconate remarked that the closer he got to the Lord, the more trouble he had with attempts by "evil powers" to affect himself and the members of his family. Ralph Martin writes: "For many of us, becoming involved in the charismatic renewal has meant not only a new experience of the Lord, but a new sensitivity to the reality and work of Satan. It is not uncommon for someone who has recently committed his life to Jesus and experienced the release of his Spirit to also experience, perhaps for the first time, the active assault of Satan in direct or subtle temptations, or in a bondage contributing to compulsive behavior. Along with this awareness of the reality of evil spirits, fortunately, has come understanding of how to deal with them."[27]

The ministry of deliverance, or of dealing with evil spirits, is made to look extremely hazardous in the motion picture, *The Exorcist*, which has been seen by millions of Americans and has been the subject of controversy among commentators and critics. There is no way of judging the extent to which this popular movie may have influenced the lives of Catholic pentecostals. It is a truth of faith for Catholics that devils, that is, "preter-human principalities and powers," exist and are operative in the world. "Since Jesus Christ overcame sin their power is only an arrogant sham,"[28] but the Church long ago took them seriously enough to institute the office of exorcist and to prescribe the prayers to be used in the rite of exorcism.

133

Older Catholics will remember the prayer to the Archangel Michael ordered by Pope Leo XIII to be recited after low Mass. This petition to Michael asked that he "be our protection against the malice and snares of the Devil," and that he, by the power of God, "cast into hell Satan and all the evil spirits who roam about the world seeking the ruin of souls." In an apparent attempt to update this tradition, Pope Paul VI, on November 15 1973, said that one of the greatest needs of the Church today is "defense from that evil which is called the Devil." He continued: "We know that this dark and disturbing spirit really exists, and that he still acts with treacherous cunning; he is the secret enemy that sows errors and misfortunes in human history."

At the present stage of development of the renewal movement, there seems to be some ambivalence about both the prevalence of evil spirits and the ministry of deliverance from them. Randy Cirner, who has commanded devils to depart from people, warns that "placing Satan at the center of all our troubles and tracing every problem to him hinders us; not everything that goes wrong in our lives is the work of evil spirits."[29] Michael Harper points out that "harm has been caused by those who seem to see Satan at work in every situation. Within the charismatic renewal there have been some crude excesses in this area. Some have been known to have a so-called 'deliverance ministry' which has brought confusion to some, and led others in defence to close the door to the real as well as to the counterfeit."[30]

Although we did not include a question about exorcism in our survey of lay Catholic charismatics, several of our respondents volunteered the information that "demon-chasing" was being introduced into their prayer groups by members who had been overly influenced by Protestant pentecostals. In our frequent attendance at prayer meetings, we never witnessed an exorcism ritual, either formal or informal, and heard only passing references to the power of evil spirits. After hearing Francis MacNutt lecture, however, and after interviewing him, we cannot doubt that there is a serious ministry of deliverance within the Catholic pentecostal movement in the United States.

Whatever skepticism the secular sociologist may bring to these miraculous and supernatural manifestations is matched by the extraordinary vigilance of the charismatic theologians, who are guarding the movement from magic and superstition. They do not want Catholic pentecostalism to be confused with adventist, spiritualist, or psychedelic expressions of religion. The best thing that the sociologist can do is to present the evidence of these collective charismatic beliefs and practices and allow the theologians to make their cautionary interpretations.

8

Afterword: Spontaneity and Routine

The sociological data we have interpreted in this study show that the cult of the Paraclete is a relatively "new" phenomenon in contemporary Catholicism, but that it is also retaining much that is "old" in the Catholic tradition.[1] The members of the cult prefer to call it a spiritual renewal that is available for all the faithful of the Church. This combination of the novel and the traditional represents the emergence of "something different" on the modern American religious scene, and it is the fact of difference in both personnel and structure that attracts the attention of the social scientist.

The flourishing and ever expanding charismatic renewal has taken the American Catholic Church by surprise. Catholic pentecostals are serene in the conviction that it is God who is responsible for the surprise. With simple faith in the Holy Spirit, they agree with Cardinal Suenens, who considers this "another instance where God chooses to work in a way that we humans would never have anticipated or chosen."[2] That this eminent European prelate came over to the United States to "learn about" Catholic pentecostalism is in itself extraordinary in light of the fact that the typical European critic tends to look on America as the most materialistic, sensate, and secular of all societies—hardly the appropriate environment for a deeply pious and devotional movement.

Counter-Culture Ideology

Much has been said and written about this post-Christian age—about the decline of religiosity and the dissolution of spiritual values in Western civilization, with America the foremost example. James Hitchcock observed in 1971 that "there is an obvious spiritual malaise affecting both religious and laymen"[3] in the Catholic Church. As recently as 1973, Andrew Greeley elicited from his research data a somber prediction concerning the "collapse" of American Catholicism. Yet, out of the heartland of affluent, technological, success-oriented America, there has emerged a remarkable religious revival that goes counter to contemporary behavioral expectations.

The second surprise is that this spontaneous and informal spiritual movement should take hold within a hierarchical, stylized, liturgical and sacramental system like Catholicism. Emotional expressions of religion had long ago been tamed, brought under control, or at least conventionalized in the Catholic Church, particularly in the Irish-Anglo version that is predominant in the United States. There was no room for outbursts of spiritual enthusiasm, spontaneous prayer and prophecy, speaking in tongues, handclapping, or the joyful singing of hymns. One would have expected to witness these activities in a revivalist tent full of Holy Rollers, but not in a Catholic church.

There had indeed been a liturgical revival that introduced

new modes of worship into the Catholic Church; it encouraged vernacular participation by the congregation, permitted guitar masses, and generally relaxed the staid and
stylized practices of the past. It too became routinized, however, with the parish priest almost always using the shortest
second Eucharistic prayer and the people substituting a
perfunctory handshake (where it was allowed at all) for the
so-called Kiss of Peace. The charismatic prayer meeting,
with or without the Eucharist, has changed all that. Intellectual understanding of the worship service—which was
expected to be the result of the English liturgy—no longer
seems as important as a warm feeling of fellowship with
both God and other human beings.

Another surprising feature of the Paraclete cult is that
it has attracted large numbers of economically comfortable,
formally educated Catholics. The pentecostal style of religion had previously been associated mainly with lower-
class Protestants of simple faith and with little formal schooling. Who would have expected the highly educated and
sophisticated faculty members of a university campus to
inaugurate the charismatic renewal among American Catholics? The chronicle is clear on this: the movement got under
way in 1967 at Duquesne University, then spread to the
University of Notre Dame, the University of Michigan, and
other centers of learning.

While the respondents to our survey do not constitute a
representative cross section of lay Catholic charismatics, we
found that about two-thirds of them had attended and/or
finished college and that relatively few of them were in
blue-collar occupations. This may be partly owing to the
fact that the early leadership came from the college campus
and the university faculty, but there appears to be nothing
inherent in the ideology and practices of the movement that

would discourage participation by those in the lower economic classes. The scarcity of black Catholics in the movement may derive from the fact that some of the better-educated black Catholics tend to identify the renewal with the "shouting" Protestant religions they have seen among poor rural blacks, and from which they dissociate themselves.

A fourth unanticipated element of the renewal movement is that it was inaugurated by lay people and remains largely under the control of the laity. In other places and at other times one might have expected the founder of a vigorous religious revival to be a pious priest or ascetic religious who had come out of monastic contemplation to crusade for the salvation of souls.[4] What may be of even greater significance is that when these lay leaders wanted to learn the "mechanics" of charismatic spirituality, they turned for counsel, not to the Catholic clergy, but to Protestant pentecostal ministers. While appreciating the approval of prelates like Cardinal Madeiros, Archbishop Hannan, and Bishop McKinney, they continue to be chary of ecclesiastical control and have no intention of being absorbed into the clerical and canonical system of the Church.[5]

It would be misleading to suggest that most Catholic pentecostals do not like priests or feel that they have no need of the clergy. In fact, many of them deplore the dearth of Spirit-filled clergy and try to convert priests to the movement. There may be some tendency toward anticlericalism among them, but this is played down when lay leaders like Paul de Celles and Kevin Ranaghan get themselves ordained to the diaconate and appear in black suits and turnaround collars. What seems to be developing here is a new and different kind of clergy-lay relationship. There is an increasingly healthy respect for priests among the laity while more and more priests are developing a mature respect for the laity. The charismatics are now being taken more seriously by the clergy and by an increasing number of previously suspicious bishops.

As a sociologist of religion, I must confess that these four characteristics of the charismatic renewal were not anticipated by the social scientists whose business it is to study collective religious trends. The experts did not foresee that a new and vigorous spiritual cult would: (a) be inaugurated by lay Catholics; (b) attract adherents from the more advantaged middle class; (c) stimulate a preference for the emotional rather than the intellectual experience of the faith; and (d) emerge in the midst of this scientistic, rational, American culture. If the Catholic hierarchy has been cautious about this singular development, the social scientists have been surprised by it.

Traditionalist Tendencies

What is happening here seems in one sense to be a manifestation of the "counter-culture," a reflection of what Charles Reich has called "Consciousness III."[6] Ordinarily we associate this concept with hippie-type youths and "street people" who reject the bourgeois conformities of American society, or with the underprivileged poor of the ghetto who are alienated from the capitalistic values of the American culture. They are sociologically notable because they do not think and act "normally"—that is, their behavior patterns differ from those that are acceptable to the majority.

It is no secret that many Catholics who are outsiders to the renewal movement look upon the charismatics as sociologically and psychologically aberrant. Even some of the priests who are now leaders and instructors in the renewal were initially repelled by "this crazy pentecostal stuff," as Gerry Ragis called it.[7] John Comer says that he first thought "these people are too happy and joyful; they must be sick, or some kind of fanatics."[8] Even George Montague says that he at first considered the baptism of the Holy Spirit a "crazy idea," and that when he finally stepped forward to be prayed over, "some of the people who prayed over me I admired greatly, but some were persons whose psychological stability I questioned."[9] In other words, the Catholic pentecostal tends to defy the expectations fostered by conventional Catholic patterns of religious expression.

Whatever the psychological peculiarities of its members, this Catholic counter-cultural movement must not be interpreted in terms of the liberal-conservative dichotomies of the larger society. The members like to insist that these words lose their meaning when a person turns to God and receives the charisms of the Holy Spirit. From the point of view of religious practices, there is certainly a "liberalizing" tendency in prayerful spontaneity and almost uninhibited spiritual enthusiasm. In terms also of some theological beliefs, the members' readiness to consort across ecumenical lines with Protestant pentecostals amounts to a liberalizing of formerly rigid orthodoxy.

Nevertheless, the Catholic pentecostals demonstrate also a definite tendency to return to the past—to traditional, Bible-centered concepts and practices—in human relations. There are two prime examples of this conservative, traditional frame of mind found among the Catholic charismatics. The first is their attitude toward the status of women, and the other is a turning away from the social action concerns that have characterized much of official church policy in recent decades. While American society is moving toward greater equality for women in all areas of life, the pentecostals are fostering a kind of biblical and, supposedly, divinely sanctioned subordination of women. While the

141

Church itself is encouraging organized crusades for social justice, the charismatics are focusing on the individual performance of the corporal works of mercy.

The majority of lay pentecostals do not want the Church to support the Women's Liberation Movement, and they are also unfavorable to the proposal that women be ordained to the priesthood. In this respect they reflect the stance of Catholic "officialdom," though probably not that of the general Catholic lay population. The more pertinent question here deals with the role and status of women within the charismatic movement itself. Approximately two-thirds of all "members," that is, people who regularly attend prayer meetings and show great enthusiasm for the movement, are women. They exert an influence that is truly charismatic and also perform those necessary and mundane ministries that are usually done by women's auxiliaries to men's organizations. Their supportive and inspirational strength is unquestionably vital to the functioning of local prayer groups.

There are well-known laywomen, like Patti Gallagher, Barbara Schlemon, and some religious sisters, who lecture at regional and diocesan conferences and promote "Antioch Weekends." Many women attend daytime prayer meetings which are organized and led by one of their number. In the highly structured Word of God covenant community at Ann Arbor, women who are designated as "handmaids" give spiritual ministry to other women, but none holds a leadership office among the community coordinators. At the top level of decision making in the national organization—the Service Committee and the Advisory Committee—it is the male voice that speaks with authority. The management and editorial direction of the movement periodical, *New Covenant*, are exclusively in male hands.

142

Whatever the participation of women in the lower eche-
lons or the auxiliary activities of the charismatic renewal,
the ideology of the movement runs counter to the general
American trend toward greater emancipation for women.
This is particularly emphasized in the pentecostal writings
and teaching on family relations, which insist on the subordination of the wife to the authority of the husband. The
theological analogy recommends that just as the Son was
in obedience to the divine Father, so also should the wife
and children be in obedience to the head of the family.[10]
This analogy appears to be the foundation for the general
charismatic attitude toward women, an attitude which is
questioned by some of the younger pentecostal feminists
in some of the less organized prayer groups. At any rate,
the movement's position on the role of women flies in the
face of contemporary American feminist ideology.

The second example of a traditionalist attitude among
Catholic charismatics is found in the area of organized
social action. This matter has been the subject of much
debate among the movement leaders—the point of contention being the nature and primary purpose of the renewal.
Bishop O'Rourke has said that his "major heartbreak has
been the failure of charismatics to make the step from
prayer to the apostolate," and he has given his message to
the movement in these words: "Get active, get involved.
Start producing fruit. I'm not sure the charismatic renewal
will last much longer unless it bears fruit."[11] The failure to
become involved in organized social action does not reflect
retrogressive attitudes toward the larger problems of the
American society among the membership. Our survey reveals
that the majority of lay pentecostals have sympathy for the
civil rights movement, the Chicano farm workers, and the
social problems of poverty, health, and housing. Less than

143

20% of them, however, have ever been actively engaged in organized movements for social reform—probably a proportion similar to that for conventional lay Catholics.

Catholic charismatics come together at their prayer meetings to praise and worship God. They have experienced a personal spiritual conversion which is symbolized in the baptism of the Spirit and expressed in witness, prophecy, and in the speaking in tongues. Members in regular attendance know each other's first names; they embrace each other joyously; they have a clear sense of fellowship as the chosen children of God. As one pentecostal priest-leader put it: "This is their purpose and calling. Why do you want them to be something else? Why do you expect them to organize on picket lines and join civil rights demonstrations and clean up City Hall?" Aside from their primary focus on prayer, the blunt and pragmatic fact is that the charismatic groups fear that they would be "torn apart" if the members attempted to find agreement on which side to take in a social controversy.

The goal of the renewal movement is personal spiritual reform, not organized social reform, but this does not imply the absence of social concern. The movement's basic conviction is that a better society can emerge only when people have become better, yet it would be completely erroneous to interpret this as an individualistic and self-centered attitude. Catholic pentecostals are deeply involved on a person-to-person basis with people who are in need. Among the New Orleans prayer groups this is an emphasized ministry—as it probably is in other places. The members are inspired to perform the corporal works of mercy: helping youths in trouble, paying rent for the poor, and visiting the lonely, the elderly, and the sick. At this level of social action and concern, the Catholic charismatic appears to be far ahead of the conventional Catholic.

Inevitable Routinization

Having reflected on the unexpected and unconventional, as well as the conservative and traditional, aspects of the pentecostal renewal, it may be well to note that the natural development of the movement, though underplayed by the charismatics, could have been foreseen by the sociologist. It is easy enough now to "reconstruct the climate," as a British sociologist does, in which the movement "took root." John Moore writes that the Vatican Council's "stress on the charismatic aspect of the church as complementary to the institutional side, the impetus it gave to historical and scriptural studies, its advocacy of ecumenism, its renewed liturgy, its declericalization of the church and its call for the layman to take an active role in church affairs, effected a profound psychological change on these Catholics—nowhere more so than in the theological departments of the universities, the starting-point and powerhouse of the whole movement."[12]

This rationalization of the cultural preliminaries to the renewal still leaves the charismatic spokesmen with the conviction that it is the surprise of the Holy Spirit, that it is God at work among His people, that it is He who leads it and keeps it going. Despite frequent protests by Catholic pentecostals that the renewal is not an organization or structure or even a movement, the original enthusiastic spontaneity has evolved into institutionalized behavior and routinized structure. The renewal is subject to the laws of development that characterize all growing social organizations. There is no way that this can be avoided short of chaos, as Francis found with his mendicant friars and Ignatius, with his contemplative actionists. The sheer multiplication of participating membership forces recognition of the need for rational organization.

The "routinization of charisma" is one of the seminal

145

sociological ideas developed by Max Weber,[13] and it is amplified and modernized in Thomas O'Dea's "paradoxes of institutionalization."[14] While the charisms of the Holy Spirit are defined as enduring gifts for both the individual and the total church, they ineluctably become repetitive behavior patterns in social collectivities. Many of their manifestations are imitative, and become learned habits of sound and gesture. We have seen that even prophecy and healing can be rationally analyzed; ways of initiating new members have been formulated and techniques for conducting successful prayer meetings carefully worked out. From one point of view, everything is left to God, but from another point of view, nothing is left to chance. These are sociological truisms and they are in no sense meant as a denial of transcendental influence and grace.

Even religious movements must become structured over a period of time, or they will cease to exist. The charismatic renewal has developed fairly clear-cut lines of leadership, power, and authority. No single individual is the elected president, or the proclaimed prophet, of the whole organization; nobody wants to assume authority, but the fact is that authority is exercised throughout the movement. At the core of the organization is the Renewal Service Committee, composed of nine men, which meets eight times a year. The Renewal Advisory Committee is made up of twenty-five men and two women. The annual National Service Conference attracts subsidiary leaders from all over the country.

A happy slogan among Catholic pentecostals is that "the only authority is the authority of service," and this is why the top management of the movement calls itself a service committee. One need only be a faithful reader of *New Covenant* to learn the names of the "movers and shakers," the chief decision makers for the whole organization.[15] There are dissenters, some of whom I have interviewed, who are not always in accord with the decisions of the national leaders, but the system of government is vaguely representative in the sense that leaders "emerge" from the membership as they display qualities of enthusiasm, competence, intelligence, and discernment. If the authority structure has to have an ecclesiastical label, it should probably be called presbyterian rather than episcopal or congregational.

This is true also at the level of the local community of charismatics, where one finds households, core groups, incipient covenant communities, leaders, and coordinators. The nomenclature has not completely gelled—what is a pastoral team in one area may be called a coordinating committee in another. Within these prayer groups there are as many ministries as there are functions to be performed or services to be rendered, and each of these ministries usually has a leader. Even though inspiration may be pure and motivation inspired, these services do not "just happen"; they result from planning, division of labor, and assignment of tasks. The success of these efforts obviously requires active organization, and one wonders why there is so much resistance to the expression of this fact in ordinary sociological terminology.

There are some peripheral structures that do not fit neatly into the organizational continuum which links the local prayer group to the national service committee. A group of young pentecostal males in Michigan is experimenting with a religious commune that may develop into a secular institute. Some Benedictines in New Mexico have established the first pentecostal abbey,[16] and a group of charismatic parents and teachers now operates a pentecostal parochial school in Providence, Rhode Island.[17] The original pentecostal parish, which was instituted in the diocese of Rockford

147

with the approval of the Bishop, appears to be the only one of its kind in the United States. The question of whether these innovations will succeed, and, perhaps, be imitated elsewhere, must remain in the realm of speculation.

A central and unsolved organizational problem still facing the pentecostal renewal in America derives from the concept of the "covenant community." The people at Ann Arbor and South Bend who control the press and the communication channels of the movement strongly support the establishment of these rigid, highly structured, and self-enclosed Christian communities. Professor Ford distinguishes communities of this kind from the many charismatic prayer groups that are loosely organized, less authoritarian, and more likely to be absorbed into the parochial level of Catholic life.[18] As yet, there has been no formal split between supporters of these two organizational concepts, and it may be that the total charismatic movement will prove broad enough to embrace both.

Notes

CHAPTER 1 (pages 1-18)

[1]H. Paul Douglass and Edmund de S. Brunner, *The Protestant Church as a Social Institution* (New York: Harper and Row, 1935), pp. 3-18. By way of contrast, they cite the fact that "the really robust Catholic mind has never hesitated to put a Pope or two in hell, because the private character of popes makes no difference to the sanctity of the church. The scientist surely can do it no greater harm."

[2]This criticism was expressed by Thomas Balduc in a letter to the editor of *Commonweal*, 8 November 1957, pp. 151-53, responding to my article, "The Sociology of Religion," *Commonweal*, 6 September 1957, pp. 558-61. For earlier criticisms by Balduc, see my book, *One-Man Research* (New York: Wiley, 1973), chap. 2, "The Dynamics of Suppression."

[3]The Fellowship subsequently changed its name to the Association for Religious Research and began in 1959 to publish the *Review of Religious Research*.

[4]Vatican II document, *Bishops' Pastoral Office in the Church*, articles 16, 17, published in Walter Abbott, ed., *The Documents of Vatican II* (New York: America Press, 1966), pp. 389-433.

[5]J. Milton Yinger, *The Scientific Study of Religion* (New York: Macmillan, 1970), pp. 1-2. See also the sociological reflections of a theologian, P. de Has, *The Church as an Institution* (Apeldoorn: Jonker, n.d.).

[6]Donald Gelpi, *Pentecostalism: A Theological Viewpoint* (Paramus: Paulist Press, 1971), p. 38.

[7]The Italian text of the Pope's words appeared in *L'Osservatore Romano*, 22 February 1973. The English translation is by Francis A. Sullivan.

[8]Cardinal Suenens attended the Conference of Charismatic Presbyterians in March 1973, and an interview with him by Ralph Martin appeared in *New Covenant*, June 1973, pp. 1-5. An excellent account of Suenens's earlier and "sociological" position may be found in Jose de Broucker, *The Suenens Dossier* (Notre

Dame: Fides, 1970). It should be remembered, however, that at Vatican II Suenens made an important statement on the charismatic aspects of the whole Church. See Hans Küng, Yves Congar, and D. O'Hanlon, eds., *Council Speeches of Vatican II* (Paramus: Paulist Press, 1964), p. 29.

[9]Edward O'Connor, *The Pentecostal Movement* (Notre Dame: Ave Maria Press, 1972), p. 29.

[10]*Ibid.*, p. 33.

[11]Catholic bookstores located in areas where pentecostal groups exist report soaring sales not only of Bibles but also of the works of mystics like Meister Eckhart, John of the Cross, and Theresa of Avila.

[12]In a research paper presented in San Francisco to the 1973 meeting of the Society for the Scientific Study of Religion, Andrew Greeley reported that approximately one-fifth of the Americans in his study have had mystical experiences.

[13]See, for example, Thomas O'Dea, "Sects and Cults," in David Sills, ed., *International Encyclopedia of the Social Sciences* (New York: Crowell, Collier and Macmillan, 1968), 14: 130-36. See also the often cited article by Virginia Hine, "Pentecostal Glossolalia: Toward a Functional Interpretation," *Journal* for the Scientific Study of Religion, Fall 1969, pp. 211-16.

[14]Stephen Clark, *Building Christian Communities* (Notre Dame: Ave Maria Press, 1972), p. 46. Clark's argument is repeated in *New Covenant,* June 1974, pp. 18-20, as an antidote to several social action articles in the same issue.

[15]Ralph Martin, *Unless the Lord Build the House* (Notre Dame: Ave Maria Press, 1971), p. 27. See also Karl Rahner, *The Christian of the Future* (New York: Herder and Herder, 1967), pp. 78-81.

[16]Andrew Greeley, *The Denominational Society* (Glenview: Scott, Foresman, 1972), chap. 6, "The Secularization Myth." See also Huston Smith, "Secularization and the Sacred: The Contemporary Scene," in Donald Cutler, ed., *The Religious Situation: 1968* (Boston: Beacon Press, 1968), pp. 583-637.

[17]Martin Marty, "The Spirit's Holy Errand: The Search for a

Spiritual Style in Secular America," in William McLoughlin and Robert Bellah, eds., *Religion in America* (Boston: Houghton Mifflin, 1968), pp. 167-83.

[18]Recognition of the "counter-culture" occurs also in John Moore, "The Catholic Pentecostal Movement," *Sociological Yearbook of Religion in Britain* 6 (London: SCM Press, 1973): 73-90. See also Joseph H. Fichter, *Community, Education and Religion* (Albany: State University of New York Press, 1972).

[19]Susan Anthony remarked that like the alcoholic, who can find an AA group wherever he goes, the Catholic pentecostal can find strength and support in any local group in the large network of charismatic communities.

[20]Meredith McGuire, "Toward a Sociological Interpretation of the 'Underground Church' Movement," *Review of Religious Research*, Fall 1972, pp. 41-47; see also her "An Interpretive Comparison of Elements of the Pentecostal and Underground Church Movements in American Catholicism," *Sociological Analysis*, Spring 1974, pp. 57-65; and Theodore Steeman, "The Underground Church," in Donald Cutler, ed., *The Religious Situation: 1969* (Boston: Beacon Press, 1969), pp. 713-48.

[21]Luther Gerlach and Virginia Hine, "Five Factors Crucial to the Growth and Spread of a Modern Religious Movement," *Journal* for the Scientific Study of Religion, Spring 1968, pp. 23-40.

[22]See the report, "Advisory Committee Meets," *New Covenant*, July 1971, pp. 7-8.

[23]See "Sociological Highlights," *New Covenant*, August 1973, p. 10. The prayer groups at Ann Arbor and South Bend were included in our original sample, but we received no response from them. Several groups led by national leaders like Jack Brombach and Fathers Gamba and MacNutt also failed to respond even after receiving follow-up letters.

[24]*New Covenant*, September 1973, p. 12.

[25]The Service Committee was later expanded to include nine members: five laymen, of whom two are deacons, and four clerics, of whom one is Bishop McKinney; *New Covenant*, February 1974, pp. 17-18.

[26]After the spectacular International Conference in June 1973, a reporter for *Time* magazine guessed that "there are probably more than 200,000 of them in the U.S. today, organized in more than 1,100 prayer groups," *Time,* 18 June 1973.

[27]The *Directory* of Catholic Charismatic Prayer Groups grew from fifty-two pages in 1972 to ninety-seven pages in 1973 and, as an added feature, listed the number of members in each group in 1973.

[28]Since only phone numbers, and no addresses, are provided in the Charismatic *Directory,* we had to check each of the 155 prayer groups against the entries in Kenedy's *Official Catholic Directory* and write to the contact person in care of the nearest parish, school, or hospital.

[29]After the "cutoff" date in early April (when we began the statistical analysis of the findings), we received twenty-one usable questionnaires. The inclusion of these would bring the response rate to 82.2%.

[30]The sixty groups led by lay contact persons represent 38% of the sample. The prayer groups led by lay people, as listed in the 1972 *Directory,* represent 67%. Had we been able to obtain addresses for all of them, we would have had 105 groups led by lay people.

[31]See Joseph H. Fichter, *Social Relations in the Urban Parish* (Chicago: University of Chicago Press, 1954), pp. 235-48.

CHAPTER 2 (pages 19-38)

[1]Ernst Troeltsch, *The Social Teachings of the Christian Churches* (New York: Harper & Row, 1960), p. 993.

[2]Howard Becker, *Systematic Sociology* (New York: Wiley, 1932), pp. 627-28.

[3]This is the thesis used to describe the development of American Methodism in Earl D. Brewer, "Sect and Church in Methodism," *Social Forces* 30 (1952): 400-408; the reverse trend in Latin American Catholicism is described in Ivan Vallier, "Roman Catholicism in Latin America: From Church to Sect," *CIF Reports* 3 (3 May 1964).

[4]Joseph H. Fichter, *Organization Man in the Church* (Cam-

bridge: Schenkman, 1974), chap. 6, "Typologies of Organized Religion."

[5]See definitions of "anamnesis," p. 19, and "cult," p. 112, in Karl Rahner and Herbert Vorgrimler, *Theological Dictionary* (New York: Herder and Herder, 1965).

[6]Troeltsch, *Social Teachings*, p. 730. See pp. 729-99 for his treatment of cults and mysticism in Protestantism; see also Werner Stark, *The Sociology of Religion* (New York: Fordham University Press, 1967), vol. 2, *Sectarian Religion*.

[7]J. Milton Yinger, *Religion, Society and the Individual* (New York: Macmillan, 1957), p. 148.

[8]N. J. Demerath and Phillip Hammond, *Religion in Social Context* (New York: Random House, 1969), p. 105.

[9]Thomas O'Dea, "Sects and Cults," in David Sills, ed., *International Encyclopedia of the Social Sciences* (New York: Crowell, Collier and Macmillan, 1968), 14:130-36. The most thoughtful analysis of the renewal as a cult is in John Moore, "The Catholic Pentecostal Movement," *Sociological Yearbook of Religion in Britain* 6 (London: SCM Press, 1973): 73-90.

[10]The Feeney side of the case is given in Catherine G. Clarke, *The Loyolas and the Cabots* (Boston: Ravengate, 1950). For a relatively sympathetic recent account see John Deedy, "Whatever Happened to Father Feeney?" *The Critic*, May-June 1973, pp. 12-24. For a sociological analysis see Thomas O'Dea, "Catholic Sectarianism," *Review of Religious Research*, 3 (1961) pp. 49-63.

[11]See the discussion of religious protest in Joachim Wach, *Sociology of Religion* (Chicago: University of Chicago Press, 1944), pp. 156-204; also Max Weber, *From Max Weber: Essays in Sociology* (New York: Oxford University Press, 1946), pp. 323-59. From the larger literature on sects see Peter Berger, "The Sociological Study of Sectarianism," *Social Research* 21 (1954): 467-87; and Bryan Wilson, "An Analysis of Sect Development," *American Sociological Review* 24 (1959): 3-15.

[12]See John T. Nichol, *Pentecostalism* (New York: Harper & Row, 1966), and Vinson Synan, *The Holiness-Pentecostal Movement* (Grand Rapids: Eerdmans, 1971).

[13]Becker, *Systematic Sociology*, p. 628.

[14]Donald Gelpi, *Pentecostalism: A Theological Viewpoint* (Paramus: Paulist Press, 1971), p. 172.

[15]Stephen Clark, *Building Christian Communities* (Notre Dame: Ave Maria Press, 1972), p. 156.

[16]Max Weber, *The Sociology of Religion* (Boston: Beacon Press, 1963), p. 46.

[17]Hans Küng, "The Charismatic Structure of the Church," in *The Church and Ecumenism* (New York: Paulist Press, 1965), 4:41-61.

[18]Ralph Keifer, "The Duquesne Weekend—1967," *New Covenant*, February 1973, p. 1.

[19]William Kolb, "Cult," in *A Dictionary of the Social Sciences*, eds. Julius Gould and William Kolb (New York: Macmillan, 1964), pp. 151-52.

[20]Some of these are discussed in Gary Rush and R. Serge Denisoff, *Social and Political Movements* (New York: Appleton-Century-Crofts, 1971), chap. 2, "Theoretical and Conceptual Approaches to Social Movements." For a more specific discussion and a good working bibliography, see Allan W. Eister, "An Outline of a Structural Theory of Cults," *Journal for the Scientific Study of Religion*, December 1972, pp. 319-33.

[21]Gelpi, *Pentecostalism*, p. 5.

[22]James Hitchcock, *The Decline and Fall of Radical Catholicism* (New York: Herder and Herder, 1971), p. 180.

[23]Apostolic Constitution, *Humanae Salutis*, in Walter Abbott, ed., *The Documents of Vatican II* (New York: America Press, 1966), pp. 703-709.

[24]See Josephine Ford, "Catholic Pentecostals," *Dialog*, Winter 1974, as condensed in *Catholic Digest*, June 1974, pp. 44-48.

[25]See *New Covenant*, August 1973, for Harold Cohen, "The Spirit of Jesus Among Us," pp. 12-13, and for Paul de Celles, "Reflections on the 1973 Conference," pp. 24-25.

[26]Edward O'Connor, *The Pentecostal Movement* (Notre Dame: Ave Maria Press, 1972), pp. 243-52.

[27]See below, Chapter 3, "Heterodoxy in Charismatic Renewal."

[28]See Paul Horton and Chester Hunt, *Sociology* (New York:

McGraw-Hill, 1964), p. 522; also, the definition of expressive movements in Herbert Blumer, "Social Movements," in Alfred M. Lee, ed., *Principles of Sociology* (New York: Barnes and Noble, 1946), p. 214.

[29]John McEleney's introduction to the Council Document on Religious Life, in Abbott, *Documents of Vatican II*, p. 464.

[30]Vatican II document, *Decree on the Appropriate Renewal of the Religious Life*, article 2. Abbott, *Documents of Vatican II*, pp. 466-82.

[31]Michael Harrison, "Sources of Recruitment to Catholic Pentecostalism," *Journal* for the Scientific Study of Religion, March 1974, pp. 49-64.

[32]Clark, *Building Christian Communities*, p. 40. Clark presents certain difficulties of terminology—he uses the word "environment" where a sociologist would use "culture" or "institutions," and the word "institution" where a social scientist would say "organization" or "group."

[33]Ralph Turner and Lewis Killian, *Collective Behavior*, 2nd ed. (Englewood Cliffs: Prentice-Hall, 1972), p. 247.

[34]Clark, *Building Christian Communities*, pp. 94 and 120. See also John Connor, "Covenant Communities: A New Sign of Hope," *New Covenant*, April 1972, pp. 2-9.

[35]These actions are described in "Advisory Committee Meets," *New Covenant*, July 1971, pp. 7-8. On January 3 1972, the committee met again. Three new priest members had been added and two priests had been dropped (one of them is not listed in the *Catholic Directory* for 1973). It was at this meeting that Bishop Joseph McKinney accepted the invitation to become Episcopal Advisor to the movement, *New Covenant*, February 1972, pp. 10-11. A more recent shift in the Advisory Committee added one brother and replaced a religious sister with a married woman, *New Covenant*, February 1974, pp. 17-18.

[36]See Joseph H. Fichter, *Religion as an Occupation* (Notre Dame: University of Notre Dame Press, 1961), "Executive Functions of Superiors." J. Massingberd Ford, in an unpublished manuscript on Catholic neo-pentecostalism, discusses the "The-

ology of Community" as operative in the charismatic renewal.

[37] *New Covenant,* July 1971, p. 8.

[38] In June 1973, *New Covenant* appeared for the first time without the subtitle, "The Monthly Magazine of the Catholic Charismatic Renewal." The change was decided upon in late April as an ecumenical gesture, the purpose being to remove "an unnecessary obstacle" to non-Catholics interested in the movement. See the editorial in *New Covenant,* June 1973.

[39] *New Covenant,* July 1973, p. 3.

[40] George Martin, "Charismatic Renewal and the Church of Tomorrow," in Kevin and Dorothy Ranaghan, eds., *As The Spirit Leads Us* (Paramus: Paulist Press, 1971), pp. 233-45. Kevin Ranaghan says that "we reject the idea that the charismatic renewal is some kind of para-ecclesiastical structure; it is not a movement which exists for itself. It is not a grouping of the elect or the wonderful spiritual elite who have been called out of a carnal dying structure" *(New Covenant,* March 1974, pp. 3-6).

CHAPTER 3 (pages 39-57)

[1] Remarks at a press conference in 1971, reported in *New Covenant,* July 1971, p. 8.

[2] Kevin M. Ranaghan, "Catholics and Pentecostals Meet in the Spirit," in Kevin and Dorothy Ranaghan, eds., *As the Spirit Leads Us* (Paramus: Paulist Press, 1971), pp. 114-44.

[3] The people who made the famous weekend retreat at Duquesne in February 1967 relied heavily on this inspirational literature. See "Charismatic Beginnings," *New Covenant,* February 1973, for this account.

[4] Remark of Bishop Joseph McKinney in an interview published in *New Covenant,* September 1971, pp. 10-16. Archbishop Dwyer's criticism appeared in the *National Catholic Register,* 21 July 1974, p. 7.

[5] Reported in Donald Gelpi, *Pentecostalism: A Theological Viewpoint* (Paramus: Paulist Press, 1971), p. 34.

[6] This term was popularized by Henry Van Dusen and later treated in scholarly fashion in William McLoughlin, "Is There

A Third Force in Christendom? " William McLoughlin and Robert Bellah, eds., *Religion in American Culture* (Homewood: Dorsey Press, 1964), pp. 45-72.

[7]Vinson Synan, "The Classical Pentecostals," *New Covenant,* May 1973, pp. 7-10, 27. McLoughlin, "Third Force," p. 67, warns that "the fringe sects are notoriously opposed to giving out their statistics partly because they have no accurate figures, partly because they fear persecution, and partly because of sheer cantankerousness toward investigators." For a more confident but controversial study see Dean M. Kelley, *Why Conservative Churches Are Growing* (New York: Harper & Row, 1972), and also the long review of this work by Charles Longino in *Journal for the Scientific Study of Religion,* December 1973, pp. 478-84.

[8]David du Plessis warned about this in 1968, "Do not conform to pentecostal patterns, for example, clapping one's hands out of imitation of the pentecostals, or raising one's arms in prayer." Quoted in Ranaghan, "Catholics and Pentecostals," p. 133.

[9]To the conventional Catholic these alien but harmless mannerisms represent what Kilian McDonnell calls "cultural baggage"; Kilian McDonnell, *Catholic Pentecostalism: Problems of Evaluation* (Pecos: Dove Publications, 1970), p. 14. To these could be added the custom of "cutting the scriptures" to discover God's will or inspiration and "laying a fleece before the Lord" as a kind of test of divine approval.

[10]Gelpi, *Pentecostalism,* p. 75.

[11]See Edward O'Connor, *The Pentecostal Movement* (Notre Dame: Ave Maria Press, 1972), chap. 8, "Dangers Inherent in Pentecostalism." See also, however, the edifying "Witnesses of Priests" in George Kosicki, ed., *The Lord Is My Shepherd* (Ann Arbor: Charismatic Renewal Press, 1973).

[12]McLoughlin, "Third Force," p. 58. See also Norman Furniss, *The Fundamentalist Controversy* (New Haven: Yale University Press, 1954), and Stewart Cole, *The History of Fundamentalism* (New York: Smith, 1931).

[13]This is by Vinson Synan, in "The Classical Pentecostals," *New Covenant,* May 1973, p. 10.

[14]Hal Lindsey, *The Late Great Planet Earth* (New York: Bantam Books, 1973). Particularly to the point is chap. 13, "The Main Event." The 1973 *Directory* of the charismatic movement lists three Catholic prayer groups as having taken the title "maranatha." They are in Sioux City, Iowa; Opelousas, Louisiana; and Salt Lake City, Utah. Here the term is probably intended as a petition—"Come, Lord Jesus!"—rather than as a prediction—"the Lord is coming soon!"

[15]Phil O'Mara, "The Return of the Lord," *New Covenant*, September 1972, pp. 2-4, 25-28. The same issue reprints an editorial, "The Lord Is Coming Again!" from *Christianity Today*, 26 June 1972, with a footnote to fundamentalist readings on the subject.

[16]Gelpi, *Pentecostalism*, p. 217.

[17]M. E. Redfor, *The Rise of the Church of the Nazarene* (Kansas City: Nazarene Publishing House, 1948), p. 42. This idea is identified as "a concept of Protestant theology" in Karl Rahner and Herbert Vorgrimler, *Theological Dictionary* (New York: Herder and Herder, 1965), p. 70.

[18]J. Massingberd Ford, *The Pentecostal Experience* (Paramus: Paulist Press, 1970), p. 48. W. Seward Salisbury, *Religion in American Culture* (Homewood: Dorsey Press, 1964), p. 164., quotes a Baptist pastor who says that his congregation believes in the "personal, pre-millenial, and imminent return of Our Lord and Savior, Jesus Christ."

[19]See "Mexican Archdiocese Issues Guidelines," *New Covenant*, August 1973, p. 27.

[20]O'Connor, *The Pentecostal Movement*, pp. 225-28.

[21]Donald Gelpi, *Pentecostal Piety* (Paramus: Paulist Press, 1972), p. 54.

[22]Guidelines and team manuals are published for these seminars.

[23]O'Connor, *The Pentecostal Movement*, p. 236.

[24]Richard Mouw, "The Evangelicals," *New Covenant*, September 1973, pp. 17-19, 30. He adds that "traditional fundamentalism has been quite hostile toward pentecostalism in its classic form, and it seems to be taking the same posture toward neopentecostalism."

25This is reminiscent of the hierarchy's opposition to the child labor amendment in the 1920's. Archbishop Lucey once told me that he was the only American Bishop who spoke in favor of it.

26Larry Christenson, "Notes on Family Life," *New Covenant,* May 1973, pp. 1-3, 27. See also Graham Pulkingham, "Headship in Christian Marriage," *New Covenant,* December 1972, p. 11. Pulkingham writes that "the revelation of Scripture is that, in a healthy relationship between husband and wife, the man is head. That's a spiritual fact. He has headship and the woman is in submission to his headship."

27Sidney Callahan, *The Illusion of Eve* (New York: Sheed and Ward, 1965), p. 92 and p. 204.

28See Barbara Morgan, "Family Life," *New Covenant,* May 1973, p. 4. John Muthing, "Pentecostalism: A Bridge to Renewal?" *St. Anthony Messenger,* September 1973, pp. 32-40, says that "many charismatics, especially those living in charismatic communities like the Word of God Community in Ann Arbor, Michigan, take the submission passage as a cardinal rule of family life."

29"Fundamentalists usually believe that the second coming of Jesus in bodily form is destined to occur in the not-too-distant future, and that desirable social changes will be introduced into our social system through this supernatural agency. Thus, social action programs do not usually receive strong endorsement from fundamentalists." Glenn Vernon, *Sociology of Religion* (New York: McGraw-Hill, 1962), p. 178.

30Edward O'Connor, *Pentecost in the Modern World* (Notre Dame: Ave Maria Press, 1972), p. 13.

CHAPTER 4 (pages 58-79)

1Ralph Martin editorial in *New Covenant,* September 1973, p. 2.

2Bert Ghezzi, "Building On Rock," *New Covenant,* September 1973, pp. 3-6, provides practical advice suggestive of the sociology of small groups.

3Interview with Dawn Gibeau, *National Catholic Reporter,* 22 June 1973, p. 15.

⁴The movement itself arose unexpectedly and spread spontaneously. "Most of those who were involved in it at the beginning found themselves taken quite by surprise." Edward O'Connor, *The Pentecostal Movement* (Notre Dame: Ave Maria Press, 1972), p. 33.

⁵The three quotations in this paragraph are from articles in *New Covenant:* Stephen Woodstock, "Rescued by Christ," June 1973, p. 17; Audrey Guillet, "A New Life with God," March 1973, p. 8; Jim Thill, "Great Is God's Mercy," April 1973, p. 14.

⁶Bobbie Cavnar, "The Power of Prayers," *New Covenant*, June 1971, p. 6. For further personal testimonies see "Bearing Witness," in Kevin and Dorothy Ranaghan, eds., *Catholic Pentecostals* (Paramus: Paulist Press, 1969), pp. 24-37, 58-106; and George Montague, *Riding the Wind* (Ann Arbor: Word of Life, 1974), pp. 1-19.

⁷Donald Gelpi, *Pentecostal Piety* (Paramus: Paulist Press, 1972), p. 95.

⁸Charles R. Meyer, *The Touch of God* (New York: Alba House, 1972), p. 63; also chap. 6, "Role of the Spirit," pp. 125-35. See also Abraham Maslow, *Toward a Psychology of Being* (New York: Van Nostrand, 1962), chap. 3.

⁹Edward O'Connor, *The Pentecostal Movement in the Catholic Church* (Notre Dame: Ave Maria Press, 1971), p. 171.

¹⁰*Acts of the Apostles*, 2/37-38.

¹¹For unsympathetic appraisals of pentecostalism, see Neils Bloch-Hoell, *The Pentecostal Movement: Its Origin, Development and Character* (Oslo: Universities forlaget, 1964), and Prudencio Damboriena, *Tongues as of Fire: Pentecostalism in Contemporary Christianity* (Washington: Corpus Books, 1969).

¹²Gelpi, *Pentecostal Piety*, p. 96. See also chapter 3 above, "Heterodoxy in Charismatic Renewal."

¹³Cardinal Suenens, "Mission for Tomorrow," homily delivered at the closing liturgy of the seventh International Conference, reported in *New Covenant*, July 1973, pp. 10-11.

¹⁴This was highlighted in a special issue, "Jesus Is Renewing All His People," *New Covenant*, May 1972, for which Baptist,

Congregational, Lutheran, Methodist, Presbyterian, and Anglican contributors wrote articles.

[15]Bernardine Abbott, letter to the editor of *America*, 27 October 1973, p. 297.

[16]"Many people are wary of the Pentecostal movement, not because of any specific points of doctrine that might be objected to, but because of a certain strangeness in the general tone or style of the spirituality which it engenders." Edward O'Connor, *The Pentecostal Movement* (Notre Dame: Ave Maria Press, 1972), p. 179.

[17]A widely circulated report of an "apparition" of the Virgin Mary at Necedah, Wisconsin, on July 2 1973 has her speaking in condemnation of both the charismatic renewal and the cursillo movement. The connection between the decline of Marian devotions and the rise of the charismatic movement is made by Richard Dalrymple, "The San Diego Catholics," *Logos Journal*, March-April 1973, pp. 53-54. On the other hand, O'Connor says that "devotion to Mary has been strengthened by the pentecostal movement." See O'Connor, *The Pentecostal Movement*, pp. 59-60, 167-68.

[18]"Mission for Tomorrow," *New Covenant*, July 1973, p. 11. A priest from Baltimore feared that the Protestant members of his prayer group would "wince" at the Cardinal's words, so he wrote an explanatory article for them. Joseph O'Meara, letter in *New Covenant*, September 1973, pp. 28-29. The revised and expanded Fall 1973 catalog from the Communication Center at Notre Dame did not include a single title on the Blessed Mother among the books, pamphlets, cassettes and record albums offered for sale.

[19]This is the subtitle of a paper, "Sources of Recruitment to Catholic Pentecostalism," presented by Michael I. Harrison at the October 1972 meeting of the Society for the Scientific Study of Religion.

[20]The "beginnings" are described in many publications, but see "Stirrings in Pittsburgh," in Kevin and Dorothy Ranaghan, *Catholic Pentecostals* (Paramus: Paulist Press, 1969), pp. 6-23.

[21]See H. Richard Niebuhr, *The Social Sources of Denomina-tionalism* (Hamden, Conn.: Shoe String Press, 1954), pp. 26-33.

[22]See Christian Lalive d'Epinay, "The Pentecostal 'Conquest' of Chile: Rudiments of a Better Understanding," in Donald R. Cutler, ed., *The Religious Situation: 1969* (Boston: Beacon Press, 1969), pp. 179-94. The study from which this essay was derived was originally titled, *El Refugio de las Masas: Estudio Socio-lógico del Protestantismo Chileno.*

[23]O'Connor, *The Pentecostal Movement,* p. 44.

[24]Their story is told in Jim Manney, "Before Duquesne: Sources of the Renewal," *New Covenant,* February 1973, pp. 12-17. See also O'Connor, *The Pentecostal Movement,* pp. 45f.

[25]See Thomas F. O'Dea, "Five Dilemmas in the Institutionali-zation of Religion," *Journal* for the Scientific Study of Religion, October 1961, pp. 32-39.

CHAPTER 5 (pages 80-98)

[1]This chapter combines and revises the contents of one article previously published, "Pentecostals: Comfort vs. Awareness," *America,* 1 September 1973, pp. 114-16, and "Liberal and Con-servative Pentecostals," to appear in *Social Compass.*

[2]J. L. and Barbara Hammond, *The Town Labourer, 1760-1832. The New Civilization* (New York: Longmans, Green, 1928), p. 224. Quoted by J. Milton Yinger, *The Scientific Study of Religion* (New York: Macmillan, 1970), p. 229.

[3]Pierre Berton, *The Comfortable Pew* (Toronto: McClelland and Stewart, 1965).

[4]Charles Glock, Benjamin Ringer, and Earl Babbie, *To Com-fort and To Challenge* (Berkeley: University of California Press, 1967), p. 6.

[5]Jeffrey Hadden, *The Gathering Storm in the Churches* (Gar-den City: Doubleday, 1969), chap. 3, "Religious and Social Beliefs."

[6]Glock, Ringer, and Babbie, *To Comfort and To Challenge,* chap. 7, "Social Ideology and Involvement."

[7]See the condensed version of his address, "The Spirit of Jesus Among Us," *New Covenant,* August 1973, pp. 12-13.

[8]Similarly, the prayer group of St. Patrick's parish in Providence, Rhode Island, holds its regular charismatic meeting on Friday nights and a separate meeting on Wednesday nights for those interested in social action. See John Randall, "Social Impact a Matter of Time," *New Covenant*, October 1972, pp. 4 and 27, and Susan Anthony, "Prayer and Social Action," *New Covenant*, February 1974, pp. 11-13.

[9]See "A Bishop's Perspective," *New Covenant*, October 1972, pp. 2-3.

[10]See Francis MacNutt, "Pentecostals and Social Justice: A Problem and A Hope," *New Covenant*, November 1972, pp. 4-6, 30-32.

[11]Donald Gelpi, *Pentecostalism: A Theological Viewpoint* (Paramus: Paulist Press, 1971), p. 5.

[12]Henri J. M. Nouwen, *Creative Ministry* (Garden City: Doubleday, 1971), pp. 78-79.

[13]The American Catholic bishops have corporately gone on record as being in opposition to the proposed Equal Rights Amendment to the Constitution, and the 1973 convention of the National Council of Catholic Women passed a resolution against ERA.

[14]See chapter 3 above, "Heterodoxy in Charismatic Renewal."

[15]It may be even more significant that the liberals are almost three times as likely (45% to 16%) as the conservatives to have attended a Catholic college or university.

[16]See the report, "Sociological Highlights," *New Covenant*, August 1973, p. 10.

[17]MacNutt, "Pentecostals and Social Justice," p. 31.

[18]Phil O'Mara, "Social Action," *New Covenant*, November 1972, pp. 13-14, 19-20.

[19]There are, however, some dramatic cases of charismatics who left the movement to join Protestant Pentecostal groups.

[20]Edward O'Connor, *The Pentecostal Movement* (Notre Dame: Ave Maria Press, 1972), p. 106.

[21]Rick Thomas, "Christmas in the Dump," *New Covenant*, May 1973, pp. 12-14; see also his article, "The Poor, The Rich, and The Kingdom," *New Covenant*, August 1973, pp. 6-9, and

Cindy Conniff, "Miracles in a Garbage Dump," *New Covenant*, April 1974, pp. 32-33.

[22]Stephen Clark, *Building Christian Communities* (Notre Dame: Ave Maria Press, 1972), p. 40.

[23]Bertil W. Ghezzi, "Three Charismatic Communities," in Kevin and Dorothy Ranaghan, eds., *As the Spirit Leads Us* (Paramus: Paulist Press, 1971), pp. 164-86. The quotation is from "Building on Rock," *New Covenant*, September 1973, pp. 3-6.

[24]James Burke, "Liberation," *New Covenant*, November 1972, pp. 1-3 and 29.

[25]MacNutt, "Pentecostals and Social Justice," p. 5.

[26]W. Graham Pulkingham is an Episcopal clergyman who is extremely popular among Catholic charismatics. In his book, *Gathered for Power* (New York: Morehouse-Barlow, 1972), he says that he was "nurtured under the rigid shadow of Irish Catholicism" (p. 37) and that in September 1951 he defected "from the Roman Catholic communion" (p. 89). For later development of social action at Pulkingham's parish, see Jeff Shiffmayer, "Is That Your School Across the Street?" *New Covenant*, January 1974, pp. 14-16.

[27]Catholic pentecostals are generally enthusiastic about the well-known American healer, Kathryn Kuhlman, an ordained Baptist minister. Her personal concern for unfortunate and afflicted people is described in the Foreword of her book, *I Believe in Miracles* (Old Tappan, N.J.: Spire Books, 1973), pp. 7-12.

[28]David Wilkerson, "Ministration or Ministry," *New Covenant*, August 1973, pp. 14-15.

CHAPTER 6 (pages 99-119)

[1]Michael I. Harrison, "Sources of Recruitment to Catholic Pentecostalism," a paper delivered at the October 1972 meeting of the Society for the Scientific Study of Religion, p. 17.

[2]Benjamin Zablocki, *The Joyful Community* (Baltimore: Penguin Books, 1971)—a book that is as much a warning as it is an encouragement for the charismatic renewal. Larry Christenson, in *A Message to the Charismatic Movement* (Minneapolis: Di-

mension Books, 1972), recounts the brief history of the now defunct Catholic Apostolic Church. It is difficult to understand what useful "message" this book has for Catholic pentecostals.

[3]Kenneth McGuire, "Affective Deprivation as a Factor in Crisis Movement Formation," paper discussed at the 1973 meetings of the Society for the Scientific Study of Religion. He takes his main concept from David Aberle, "A Note on Relative Deprivation Theory as Applied to Millenarian and Other Cult Movements," in W. Lessa and E. Vogt, eds., *Reader in Comparative Religion* (New York: Harper & Row, 1968), pp. 527-31.

[4]The annual *Directory* of Catholic charismatic groups lists under each group the percentage of Catholic membership. In this study we have contacted only Catholic respondents in groups with a majority of Catholic members.

[5]Only 14% said that they had invited non-Catholics to join the Church. Several respondents thought we should have asked, "How many Catholics have you invited to join the charismatic renewal?"

[6]Harrison, "Sources of Recruitment," p. 11, reports that 61% of his respondents in the Ann Arbor group are females.

[7]Sue Manney, "Alone in the Spirit," *New Covenant,* October 1973, pp. 17-19; she adds the subtitle, "the problems of a husband or wife involved in the renewal without his partner."

[8]The demand for total commitment of members to religious sects is discussed in J. Milton Yinger, *Religion in the Struggle for Power* (Durham: Duke University Press, 1946), pp. 22-23; and, especially, in Lewis Coser, "Greedy Organizations," *Archives Europeenes de Sociologie* (Waltham, Mass.: Brandeis University, 1967), pp. 196-215.

[9]The content of this section was previously reported by the author in "Women in Charismatic Renewal," *National Catholic Reporter,* 28 September 1973.

[10]Sue Manney, "Alone in the Spirit," p. 17. See also the two-part article by the Presbyterian minister Brick Bradford, "Divine Order in Christian Marriage," *New Covenant,* January 1974, pp. 3-7, and February 1974, pp. 19-23.

[11]In an interview with one of the handmaids at Ann Arbor, I learned that some of the younger female members are not entirely satisfied with the subordinate role of women in the community.

[12]Mary Papa, "People Having a Good Time Praying," *National Catholic Reporter,* 17 May 1967.

[13]Kevin and Dorothy Ranaghan, *Catholic Pentecostals* (Paramus: Paulist Press, 1969), pp. 24-37, 58-106.

[14]Kevin and Dorothy Ranaghan, eds., *As the Spirit Leads Us* (Paramus: Paulist Press, 1971).

[15]J. Massingberd Ford, *The Pentecostal Experience* (Paramus: Paulist Press, 1970).

[16]See the description by Mary Maureen in, "Focus: A Daytime Prayer Group," *New Covenant,* March 1974, pp. 16-18.

[17]The story has been told and retold, but see the special issue of *New Covenant,* "Charismatic Beginnings, 1967," February 1973, and particularly the article by Jim Manney, "Before Duquesne: Sources of the Renewal," pp. 12-17.

[18]The content of this section is from a paper, "Priests and Renewal," presented to a group of American Jesuit priests at the 1973 Charismatic Conference at Notre Dame.

[19]Edward O'Connor, *The Pentecostal Movement in the Catholic Church* (Notre Dame: Ave Maria Press, 1971), p. 237.

[20]George Martin, "Charismatic Renewal and the Church of Tomorrow," in Ranaghan and Ranaghan, *As the Spirit Leads Us,* pp. 233-45.

[21]"The Layman is on the move. Yes, thank God, after centuries of watching the Church, he has realized that he is the Church"; Ranaghan and Ranaghan, *Catholic Pentecostals,* p. 241.

[22]A precise count of the 536 prayer groups listed in the 1972 *Directory* shows that a priest was the contact person for 27% of them.

[23]The June 1972 issue of *New Covenant* was called "Priests and Holy Spirit," and featured articles by three priests who gave witness of their own "conversion."

[24]Joseph McKinney, "An Open Letter to Priests," *New Covenant,* June 1972, pp. 8-9.

[25]This priest had been praised by his bishop as having "the proper theological background to give proper direction to the large number of people who are becoming involved in the charismatic movement in this diocese." See "National News," *New Covenant*, January 1973, p. 23.

[26]O'Connor, *Pentecostal Movement in the Catholic Church*, p. 253.

[27]Donald Gelpi calls for clergy leadership on the local as well as the diocesan level of the Church, and says, "It is imperative that more members of the Catholic theological community emerge from their academic ghetto and provide solid, competent, and creative reflection upon a major religious phenomenon in the life of the American Church." Donald Gelpi, *Pentecostal Piety* (Paramus: Paulist Press, 1972), p. 54.

[28]The brief papal statement is reprinted in *New Covenant*, December 1973, p. 5. Commentators chose to ignore the authoritarian tone of this message.

[29]Reported by Jim Manney in, "International Conference," *New Covenant*, July 1973, p. 6.

[30]Harold Cohen, "The Spirit of Jesus Among Us," *New Covenant*, August 1973, pp. 12-13.

[31]Paul de Celles, "Reflections on the 1973 Conference," *New Covenant*, August 1973, pp. 24-25.

[32]O'Connor, *Pentecostal Movement in the Catholic Church*, p. 91, explains that "the bishop had not ordered priests to withdraw from the movement, but merely wanted them to avoid roles of active leadership which might give the impression that the movement had been officially approved by the Church."

[33]This report was submitted by Bishop Alexander Zaleski to the Washington meeting of the American Bishops on 14 November 1969.

[34]Personal correspondence from Bishop McKinney, dated 23 March 1973. Among the forty-three bishops who approve the movement, twenty-four had appointed diocesan moderators. Among the remaining forty-five, only sixteen had done so.

[35]This is included in the "problem areas" described by Kilian McDonnell and his associates in their "Statement of the Theo-

logical Basis of the Catholic Charismatic Renewal," published as "News" in *New Covenant,* January 1974, pp. 21-23.

CHAPTER 7 (pages 120-135)

[1]The sociologist of religion does not hesitate to say that "the personal subjective relationship of man with the Beyond is at the very heart of religious life. . . . The relationship of the individual to the Beyond is the substance of personal faith." See Thomas and Janet O'Dea, *Readings on the Sociology of Religion* (Englewood Cliffs: Prentice-Hall, 1973), p. 37.

[2]See the entry under "prophet," in Karl Rahner and Herbert Vorgrimler, *Theological Dictionary* (New York: Herder and Herder, 1965), p. 384. This does not contradict the statement of Vatican II in the *Constitution on Divine Revelation,* art. 4: "We now await no further new public revelation before the glorious manifestation of our Lord Jesus Christ."

[3]The full texts of these two brief prophecies appear as "God's Word to Us," with the editorial statement that "in response to numerous requests, we print them here for your prayerful consideration," *New Covenant,* October 1973, p. 23.

[4]Donald Gelpi, *Pentecostalism: A Theological Viewpoint* (Paramus: Paulist Press, 1971), pp. 149-50.

[5]Bruce Yocum's three-part discussion, "Prophecy," appears in *New Covenant,* June 1973, pp. 26-27; July, pp. 12-14; August, pp. 19-22.

[6]*Ibid.,* p. 20.

[7]Gelpi, *Pentecostalism,* p. 136.

[8]See John Sherill, *They Speak with Other Tongues* (Old Tappan, N.J.: Revell, 1973), pp. 100-102.

[9]George Montague, however, sang in tongues over a religious sister who then said: "Some of your words I recognized as words of the Sioux dialect my grandmother used to speak." George Montague, *Riding the Wind* (Ann Arbor: Word of Life, 1974), p. 18.

[10]J. Massingberd Ford, *The Pentecostal Experience* (Paramus: Paulist Press, 1970), p. 35.

¹¹This contradicts Yocum's claim of having heard a number of prophecies in which the Lord said, "I am coming very soon." Yocum, "Prophecy," p. 22.

¹²Kilian McDonnell, *Catholic Pentecostalism: Problems in Evaluation* (Pecos: Dove Publications, 1970), p. 33.

¹³See chapter 3 above, "Heterodoxy in Charismatic Renewal."

¹⁴Mary Ann Jahr, "The Second Lutheran Conference," *New Covenant*, October 1973, pp. 10-11.

¹⁵Ralph Martin, "David Wilkerson's Vision," *New Covenant*, January 1974, pp. 11-12.

¹⁶David du Plessis, "Persecution for Charismatic Catholics?" *New Covenant*, January 1974, p. 13. See also Lorraine Juliana, who warns that Wilkerson "is proclaiming a message of new division, of separation, of fear and distrust," *New Covenant*, March 1974, p. 37.

¹⁷Martin, "David Wilkerson's Vision," p. 12.

¹⁸"Roman Catholics who have no problem with accepting a healing at Lourdes or Fatima sometimes are hesitant to even admit the possibility of a healing through a charism of the Holy Spirit. While they would consider it a mark of piety to seek a cure at Lourdes they would think it an expression of hysteria to seek a cure through a charism of the Holy Spirit." McDonnell, *Catholic Pentecostalism*, p. 21.

¹⁹Editorial in *New Covenant*, November 1973, p. 3.

²⁰Ford, *The Pentecostal Experience*, p. 42.

²¹Agnes Sanford, *The Healing Light* (Watchung, N.J.: Macalester, 1972), chap. 11, "The Healing of the Emotions." Barbara Schlemon, who is active in the healing ministry, says she learned this method of prayer from Agnes Sanford; see "The Healing of the Inner Man," *New Covenant*, May 1974, pp. 7-10.

²²Francis MacNutt, "The Inner Healing of Our Emotional Problems," *New Covenant*, May 1974, pp. 3-6. See also his book, *Healing* (Notre Dame: Ave Maria Press, 1974).

²³Gelpi, *Pentecostalism*, p. 154.

²⁴Kathryn Kuhlman's prestige is high among Catholic pentecostals, partly as a result of her having been received in audience

by Pope Paul VI. Her book, *I Believe in Miracles* (Old Tappan, N.J.: Revell, 1969), is even more popular among charismatics than Agnes Sanford's *The Healing Light.*

[25]Francis MacNutt, "Four Kinds of Healing," *New Covenant,* March 1974, pp. 29-30. He writes further on "Deliverance and Exorcism" in his book, *Healing,* pp. 208-31.

[26]Michael Harper, *Spiritual Warfare* (Watchung, N.J.: Charisma Books, 1971), chap. 11, "Defeating the Enemy." Under the same title excerpts from this book were published in *New Covenant,* April 1974, pp. 10-11. Harper is now a contributing editor to this periodical.

[27]Ralph Martin, "Confronting the Reality of Satan," *New Covenant,* April 1974, p. 3.

[28]See the definitions for "devils, demons," pp. 126-27, and "possession," p. 365, in Rahner and Vorgrimler, *Theological Dictionary.*

[29]Randy Cirner, "Deliverance," *New Covenant,* April 1974, pp. 4-7, and May 1974, pp. 22-25. These reflections grew out of the seminar on the same subject Cirner conducted at the 1973 Charismatic Conference at Notre Dame. At the same Conference there was a workshop on the occult conducted by Paul and Mary Gray, and a seminar on the occult by Rob Ellerby and Fred Gumina.

[30]Harper, *Spiritual Warfare,* p. 13.

CHAPTER 8 (pages 136-148)

[1]This afterword is a revision of an article, "How It Looks to a Social Scientist," *New Catholic World,* November-December, 1974, pp. 244-48.

[2]Ralph Martin's interview with Cardinal Suenens, *New Covenant,* June 1973, pp. 1-5. The issue was entitled "The Surprises of the Holy Spirit."

[3]James Hitchcock, *The Decline and Fall of Radical Catholicism* (New York: Herder and Herder, 1971), p. 180. He cites Michael Novak's remark that "in pragmatic, secular America it is almost impossible for a religious faith to take intelligent root."

⁴It is often pointed out, however, that neither Francis of Assisi nor Ignatius Loyola was a priest when he successfully inspired religious renewal within the Church.

⁵Cardinal Umberto Madeiros of Boston publicly encouraged his clergy to become involved in the charismatic renewal. He is the highest ranking American prelate to support the movement. See his letter to the priests of the archdiocese in *The Pilot*, 1 March 1974.

⁶Charles Reich, *The Greening of America* (New York: Random House, 1970). See also Theodore Roszak, *The Making of a Counter-Culture* (Garden City: Doubleday, 1969).

⁷See his contribution in George Kosicki, ed., *The Lord Is My Shepherd* (Ann Arbor: Charismatic Renewal, 1973), pp. 73-78.

⁸*Ibid.*, pp. 17-20. This book contains the "witnesses" of thirteen priests and the "Open Letter to Priests" from Bishop Joseph McKinney.

⁹George Montague, *Riding the Wind* (Ann Arbor: Word of Life, 1974), p. 15.

¹⁰"No matter how deep her insight may be, a woman must be in submission to her husband just as Christ is submissive to the Father, perfectly obedient in all things. . . . When a woman submits to her husband and acknowledges his headship, she is submitting to the will of God." Sue Manney, "Alone in the Spirit," *New Covenant,* October 1973, pp. 17-19.

¹¹See also the other critical comments in "Interview with Bishop O'Rourke," *New Covenant*, October 1973, pp. 15-16. Interestingly enough, the "Readers' Response" column in subsequent issues carried no answers to the Bishop's criticisms. A kind of response, however, came in a special issue of *New Covenant*, June 1974, which contained several articles on social problems, two of them by black Protestant clergymen.

¹²John Moore, in "The Catholic Pentecostal Movement," *Sociological Yearbook of Religion in Britain* 6 (London: SCM Press, 1973): 73-90, observes also that "America, a fertile breeding ground of enthusiastic movements, is given to periodic religious revivals."

[13]See the pertinent excerpts from Max Weber, "Charisma: Its Revolutionary Character and its Transformation," in Norman Birnbaum and Gertrud Lenzer, eds., *Sociology and Religion* (Englewood Cliffs: Prentice-Hall, 1969), pp. 184-96.

[14]Thomas O'Dea, "Five Dilemmas in the Institutionalization of Religion," *Journal* for the Scientific Study of Religion, Spring 1961, pp. 30-39.

[15]At the end of 1973 fourteen charismatic leaders were named as contributing editors to *New Covenant*, nine of them Protestants. Three months later Ralph Martin announced the appointment of four "international" consultants, from Belgium, Mexico, Puerto Rico, and Australia, to his International Communication Office.

[16]Mary Ann Jahr, "The First Pentecostal Abbey," *New Covenant*, May 1974, pp. 20-21.

[17]Reported in the *Wall Street Journal*, 12 March 1974, pp. 1, 35.

[18]J. Massingberd Ford, "Catholic Pentecostals," *Catholic Digest*, June 1974, pp. 44-48, condensed from *Dialog*, Winter 1974.

Appendix

CHARISMATIC RENEWAL STUDY
Loyola University of the South
New Orleans, Louisiana 70118

NOTE: This is for ADULT CATHOLIC LAITY: *NOT* for Priests, Religious,
Students, Seminarians, Non-Catholics

1. Father Harold F. Cohen, S. J. says that "Charismatic Renewal is one
   of the fastest growing movements in the Church around the world
   today." With his encouragement, we want to find out more about
   the *adult Catholic laity* who are active in this movement — their
   experiences, aspirations and ideas.

2. You will be very helpful — and charitable — if you answer these
   questions as frankly and clearly as you can. There is no need to
   identify yourself. The responses will be handled only statistically
   after being punched on IBM cards and then transferred to electronic
   tapes.

3. Please read every item carefully — and give your best answer rather
   than skip any of them. Much of the reliability of this study depends
   on the completeness of every questionnaire. You can probably do it
   in less than twenty minutes.

4. Most questions can be answered by a quick check off in the appropriate ( ) parenthesis, or by circling a number or letter. Some may
   require write-in answers like this:

173

In what Church Parish do you presently reside? _____

5. Where does your Prayer Group most often hold its meetings?
   1. ( ) Own Home Parish   2. ( ) Another Parish
   3. ( ) Elsewhere: _____

6. Are you now, or have you ever been, active in any regular parish group (other than Charismatic Renewal)?
   1. ( ) Yes, am now   2. ( ) Used to be   3. ( ) No

7. How often do you attend Sunday Mass (or Saturday evening) in your Parish Church?
   1. ( ) Every week   4. ( ) Occasionally
   2. ( ) Two or three times a month   5. ( ) Hardly ever
   3. ( ) Once a month

8. Do you look upon your home parish as a genuine Christian Community?
   1. ( ) Very much so   2. ( ) Somewhat   3. ( ) Hardly at all
   4. ( ) Not at all

9. During the past year has any priest from your parish been in your home?
   1. ( ) No   2. ( ) Yes, once   3. ( ) Several times   4. ( ) Often

10. When did you begin attending Charismatic Renewal meetings?
                   Month:_____ Year:_____

11. Your Sex: 1. ( ) Layman   2. ( ) Laywoman   And Race:_____

12-13. Your age at last birthday: ___ years old

14-15. Are you a convert to Catholicism? If so, at what age?___ years of age.

16-21. Here are some of the principal benefits that come to people from the Charismatic Renewal. Please rate them in importance to you. Write in the numbers from 1 to 6 in order of importance.

	Rank
16. A sense of close community in the Prayer Group	( )
17. Appreciation of God's special goodness to me	( )
18. A genuine conviction of my personal salvation	( )
19. Greater love for my fellow human beings	( )
20. A feeling of God's presence in my everyday life	( )
21. A sense of freedom from institutional religion	( )

22. What is your present marital status:
    1. ( ) Single (never married)   4. ( ) Separated from a Catholic
    2. ( ) Married to a Catholic   5. ( ) Separated from a non-
    3. ( ) Married to a non-Catholic   Catholic
                             6. ( ) Widowed of a Catholic
                             7. ( ) Widowed of a non-
                                  Catholic

23-25. How much education did you and your parents have?

	Yourself	Father	Mother
1. ( ) Did not finish elementary school	( )	( )	( )
2. ( ) Completed eighth grade	( )	( )	( )
3. ( ) Had some high school	( )	( )	( )
4. ( ) Graduated from high school	( )	( )	( )
5. ( ) Had some college	( )	( )	( )
6. ( ) Graduated from college	( )	( )	( )

25. Circle number of years you attended Catholic elementary school:
                           0 1 2 3 4 5 6 7 8

26-27. Circle number of years you attended Catholic high school:
                                  0 1 2 3 4
             And Catholic college: 0 1 2 3 4

28. Among your three closest friends (*not* spouse or relative) how many are Catholic?
    1. ( ) Only one   2. ( ) Two   3.( ) All three
    4. ( ) None of them

29. Among these three closest friends how many attend Charismatic Prayer Meetings?
    1. ( ) Only one   2. ( ) Two   3. ( ) All three
    4. ( ) None of them

30. Which of the following terms best fits the economic status of yourself and your family?
    1. ( ) Fairly well off   3. ( ) Middle income
    2. ( ) Above average income 4. ( ) Below average
                             5. ( )We are poor people

31. If you are gainfully employed, what is your job or occupation? (If you are a "non-working" wife, what does your husband do?) _____

32. Did you ever consider the priesthood or religious life for yourself?
    1. ( ) No, never thought of it
    2. ( ) Considered it, but not seriously
    3. ( ) Considered it seriously but decided against it
    4. ( ) Actually entered the seminary (or postulancy or novitiate or convent) but left after _____ years

33-41. Here are some issues of current interest to American Catholics. How do you feel about them? (Please check each item)

	Approve	Am neutral	Dis- approve	Don't know
33. Higher social welfare payments	( )	( )	( )	( )
34. Use of the pill by married women	( )	( )	( )	( )
35. Racially integrated schools	( )	( )	( )	( )
36. Optional marriage for priests	( )	( )	( )	( )
37. Negro Civil Rights Movement	( )	( )	( )	( )
38. The Medicare program	( )	( )	( )	( )
39. Laws for open housing	( )	( )	( )	( )
40. Popular election of bishops	( )	( )	( )	( )
41. Minimum wage of $2 per hour	( )	( )	( )	( )

42-53. Here are various statements about religion. To what degree do you agree or disagree? SA = Strongly Agree; A = Agree; D = Disagree; SD = Strongly Disagree. (Circle the letter nearest your own belief)

42. The Spirit speaks to the heart — not the mind   SA   A   D   SD

43. Priests have a place on picket lines   SA   A   D   SD

44. I have received the Baptism of the Spirit   SA   A   D   SD

45. Since lay people receive the gifts of the Spirit, Charismatic Renewal could go on without the clergy   SA   A   D   SD

46. The Church should lead in social protest movements   SA   A   D   SD

47. I have received the gift of speaking in tongues   SA   A   D   SD

48. Christ is truly present in the Eucharist   SA   A   D   SD

49. Accepting Jesus as my personal Savior means that I am already saved   SA   A   D   SD

50. The Second Coming of Christ is imminent   SA   A   D   SD

51. The Church should support Women's Liberation.   SA   A   D   SD

52. Pope Paul VI is the infallible Vicar of Christ   SA   A   D   SD

53. I know how it feels to repent and experience the forgiveness of sins   SA   A   D   SD

54. If the Bishop were to prohibit Charismatic Renewal meetings in this diocese, would you be inclined to:
   1. (   ) Simply ignore his prohibition
   2. (   ) Continue meetings while trying to persuade him otherwise
   3. (   ) Discontinue but try to get him to change his mind
   4. (   ) Simply follow his orders

55-63. Since becoming active in the Charismatic Renewal Movement have you done the following things more often, or less often, than you used to? (Please check off every item.)

	More often	Less often	No change	Never did
55. Asked a non-Catholic to join the Church	( )	( )	( )	( )
56. Visited the Blessed Sacrament	( )	( )	( )	( )
57. Read the Scriptures	( )	( )	( )	( )
58. Personally gave help to poor people	( )	( )	( )	( )
59. Received Holy Communion	( )	( )	( )	( )
60. Attended Holy Mass	( )	( )	( )	( )
61. Prayed the Rosary	( )	( )	( )	( )
62. Contributed money to my home parish	( )	( )	( )	( )
63. Gone to Confession	( )	( )	( )	( )

64-72. Are you now, or were you ever, active in the following "movements," or forms of group activities? (Please check each one.)

	Am now	Used to be	Never was
64. Voter registration campaign	( )	( )	( )
65. Christian Family Movement	( )	( )	( )
66. The Block Rosary	( )	( )	( )
67. Anti-War demonstration	( )	( )	( )
68. Cursillo Movement	( )	( )	( )
69. An "underground" Church	( )	( )	( )
70. Grape or lettuce boycott	( )	( )	( )
71. Interracial movement	( )	( )	( )
72. Conference of Christians and Jews	( )	( )	( )

FINAL NOTE: If you have any comments please feel free to add them here.

Thank you very much for taking the trouble to answer this questionnaire. May the Lord bless you and keep you close to Himself. Praise the Lord!

Index

180

Joseph H. Fichter, S. J. is Professor of Sociology at Loyola University in New Orleans, Louisiana. He holds his Ph.D. from Harvard University and two honorary degrees, a D.Litt. from Spring Hill College and a Doctor of Laws from Marquette University. He has been a visiting professor at the University of Muenster in Germany, Notre Dame, Fordham, the University of Chile in Santiago, Sir George Williams University in Montreal, and the University of Chicago. From 1965 to 1970 he held the Chauncey Stillman Chair at Harvard University. He is the author of *One Man Research: Reminiscences of a Catholic Sociologist; Organization Man in the Church; Religion as an Occupation; Social Relations in the Urban Parish; America's Forgotten Priests;* and many other books.

DATE DUE

GAYLORD | | | PRINTED IN U.S.A.